The

Sierra Tucson Cookbook

RECIPES FOR A
NEW HEALTHSTYLE™

The *Sierra Tucson Cookbook*

RECIPES FOR A NEW HEALTHSTYLE™

Written by
the Nutritional Services Staff
at Sierra Tucson

Illustrated By
Linda Dugan

Published by
Sierra Tucson Educational Materials

Published by

STEM Publications
P.O.Box 8307
Tucson, Arizona 85738
(602) 792-5819
(800) 521-7836

ISBN 0-922641-81-1

Table of Contents

Acknowledgements

Our patients and their family members provided the original impetus for this book with their many requests for recipes.

Bill O'Donnell continues to provide support and direction for all Sierra Tucson projects.

Emily Mason has provided the structure and guidance that have made this book possible.

Cathryn Matthes, Sierra Tucson Chef Manager, has provided recipes for this collection and has greatly influenced the style and presentation of the meals at Sierra Tucson.

We would also like to thank and acknowledge the following people for their contributions:

Jim Belanger
Sharon Carpenter
Ellen Duperret
Mary Lyons
Christine Troska
Ralf Weber
Debbie Wold
Gael Stirler
Lynn Bishop
Linda Dugan
Jeanette Egan

Welcome

*S*ierra Tucson has always considered nutrition an essential part of its treatment program. Our goal has been to provide a healthy way of eating by offering healthy foods that can be included as part of the recovery process.

As a result of requests from many patients and family members, we have published this cookbook that includes recipes for foods that have been served at our facilities. Most of the recipes are low in fat and the foods requiring a sweetener are sweetened with more natural "sugars." We have included some recipes which are not low in fat and we recommend that you serve these less frequently. All of the recipes include food "exchanges" in a serving to assist anyone on a food plan.

We hope you will enjoy these recipes as much as our patients have and that the recipes can be an important part of your recovery.

Breakfast & Brunch

MUESLI

Preheat oven to 350°F. Combine oats, oat bran, cinnamon, honey, and almonds in a medium-size bowl. Spread thinly on a baking sheet and bake about 10 minutes or until golden. Cool and add the bran flakes. Refrigerate or freeze. Add grated apple before serving.

YIELD 8 (1/2-cup) servings
1 serving = 2 starches and 1 fat (with almonds)
1 serving = 2 starches (without almonds)

1 cup rolled oats
1 cup oat bran
1/4 teaspoon ground cinnamon
1/2 cup honey
1/2 cup sliced almonds (optional)
1 cup whole-bran flakes
1 cup grated apple

3

YOGURT

Blend water and milk powder in a small saucepan. Cook over medium heat until milk is scalded (tiny bubbles form around edge of pan). Add to skim milk. Cool to 110°F. Stir in yogurt starter with a sterilized utensil. Pour into a sterile 1/2 gallon glass jar. Cover loosely and place in an oven preheated to 100°F with the door open 4 hours. In a gas oven, use pilot heat only.

1-3/4 cups water
3/4 cup nonfat dry milk powder
1 quart skim milk
1 tablespoon yogurt starter

YIELD 6 (1-cup) servings
1 serving = 1 milk

HINT
Sterilize utensils and jar by pouring boiling water over them or dipping them into boiling water. Allow to air dry on clean paper towels.

FRUITED YOGURT

Combine yogurt, jam, and fruit, if using, in a small bowl.

YIELD 1 (1-1/2-cup) serving

1 serving = 1 dairy and 1 fruit

1 cup plain nonfat yogurt

1/2 cup Simple Fruit Jam (page 8) or other jam made without sugar

Fresh chopped fruit (optional)

SMOOTHIES

Combine all ingredients except skim milk in a blender and blend 2 minutes. Add skim milk to thin if necessary. Pour into glasses.

YIELD 2 (1-cup) servings

1 serving = 1/2 milk and 1 fruit

1 cup plain nonfat yogurt

1 cup fruit juice (apple, orange, or pineapple)

2 tablespoons protein powder (page 171)

1 very ripe banana

1/2 cup seasonal fruit such as strawberries, orange, pineapple, papaya, or blueberries

1/2 teaspoon of one of these spices—ground cinnamon, nutmeg, allspice, coriander, or 1/8 teaspoon ground cloves;

or 1/2 teaspoon almond, vanilla, or mint extract

Skim milk (if necessary)

HINT

Favorite combinations made from fresh fruits are strawberry-orange, pineapple-papaya, or pineapple-blueberry.

COTTAGE-CHEESE PANCAKES

Put cottage cheese in a blender or food processor fitted with the metal blade and process until smooth. Add egg and egg whites and process until blended. Add flour and oil. Blend just until mixed. Spray a nonstick griddle with nonstick cooking spray and heat over medium heat. Using 1/4 cup batter for each pancake, pour batter onto hot griddle. Cook pancakes until bubbles form on surface. Turn and cook about 2 more minutes or until firm and well browned. Serve with unsweetened fruit.

1 cup lowfat cottage cheese

1 egg

4 egg whites

1/4 cup whole-wheat flour

1 tablespoon vegetable oil

YIELD 8 small pancakes
1 pancake = 1 protein

HINT

Beat leftover egg yolks in a container with 1 teaspoon lemon juice. Yolks may be used to make mayonnaise, Caesar dressing, hollandaise sauce, or used in other recipes (Raspberry Vinaigrette, page 27, or Tarragon Dipping Sauce, page 38). Yolks will keep refrigerated 2 to 3 days.

$\mathcal{S}$IMPLE FRUIT JAM

4 cups fresh or
   frozen fruit
   (2 cups when
   thawed or
   mashed)

1/2 cup water

2 tablespoons
   cornstarch

2 tablespoons cold
   water

2 to 4 tablespoons
   granulated
   fructose

Place fruit and the 1/2 cup of water in a small saucepan and bring to a simmer. Cook over medium heat 3 minutes, stirring occasionally. Combine cornstarch and the 2 tablespoons of water in a cup and stir with a fork until all lumps are dissolved. Gently stir cornstarch mixture into the simmering fruit with a spoon. Stirring constantly, bring back to a simmer and simmer 10 seconds. Remove from heat. Stir in fructose to taste. Use the jam hot on pancakes or waffles, or cold on sandwiches.

YIELD 3 cups or 48 (1-tablespoon) servings

1 serving = 1 free exchange

HINT

Strawberries or blueberries require less fructose than raspberries or blackberries. Try different berry mixtures. If you prefer the fruit chunky, cook less and do not stir as much.

8

CHILE RELLENOS CASSEROLE

Preheat oven to 350°F. Brown beef and onion in a medium-size skillet, stirring to break up meat, and drain off fat. Sprinkle meat with salt and pepper. Place 1/2 of the chiles in a 10″ x 6″ baking dish. Sprinkle with 1/2 of the cheese; top with meat mixture. Arrange remaining chiles over meat. Top with the remaining cheese. Combine remaining ingredients in a medium-size bowl. Beat mixture until smooth. Pour over all. Bake 45 to 50 minutes or until a knife inserted in center comes out clean. Cool 5 minutes. Cut into squares.

YIELD 8 servings

1 serving = 3 proteins

1 pound lean ground beef

1/2 cup chopped onion

1/2 teaspoon salt

1/4 teaspoon pepper

2 (4-oz.) cans green chiles, cut into strips

1-1/2 cups shredded lowfat Cheddar cheese (about 6 oz.)

1-1/2 cups skim milk

1/4 cup unbleached all-purpose flour

1/2 teaspoon each salt and pepper

4 eggs, beaten

Hot pepper sauce to taste

9

CRUSTLESS QUICHE

2 cups chopped
  vegetables
  (bell pepper,
  onion, zucchini,
  artichoke hearts,
  yellow squash,
  mushrooms, etc.)
1 cup shredded
  lowfat cheese
  (4-oz.)
18 egg whites
1 cup skim milk
1/4 cup grated
  Parmesan cheese

Preheat oven to 350°F. Spray a 13″ x 9″ baking dish with nonstick cooking spray. Spread chopped vegetables in baking dish. Top with lowfat cheese. Combine egg whites and milk in a medium-size bowl. Pour over vegetables and cheese. Sprinkle with Parmesan cheese. Bake, uncovered, 50 to 60 minutes or until top is browned and quiche is set.

YIELD 6 servings

1 serving = 3 lean proteins

SPINACH SOUFFLÉ

Preheat oven to 325°F. Spray a 9-inch square baking dish with nonstick cooking spray. Cook onions and spinach in their juices until onions are softened; remove from heat. Blend in cream cheese. Combine eggs, milk, and half and half in a large bowl. Season with salt, white pepper, nutmeg, and dill weed. Spread spinach mixture in prepared dish. Pour egg mixture over spinach mixture. Top with buttered bread crumbs. Bake 30 minutes or until set.

YIELD 8 servings

1 serving = 2 proteins, 1 vegetable, and 3 fats

1/2 medium-size onion, minced

2 green onions, finely chopped

1 (8-oz.) package frozen chopped spinach, thawed, drained

1 (8-oz.) package reduced-fat cream cheese

8 eggs, slightly beaten

3 cups 2% milk

1 cup half and half

Salt and white pepper to taste

1/4 teaspoon grated nutmeg

1 tablespoon dill weed

1 cup buttered bread crumbs (1/4 cup melted margarine mixed with 1 cup dry bread crumbs)

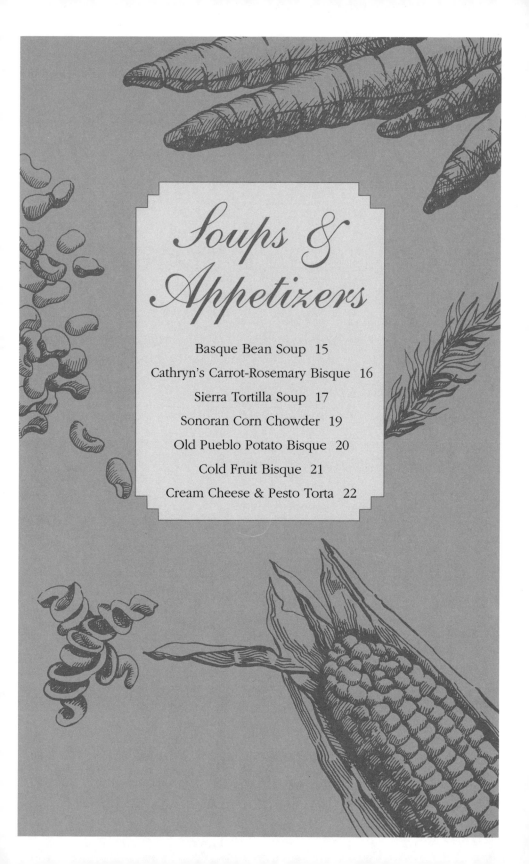

Soups &
Appetizers

Basque Bean Soup 15

Cathryn's Carrot-Rosemary Bisque 16

Sierra Tortilla Soup 17

Sonoran Corn Chowder 19

Old Pueblo Potato Bisque 20

Cold Fruit Bisque 21

Cream Cheese & Pesto Torta 22

BASQUE BEAN SOUP

1/4 cup vegetable oil

1/2 medium-size onion, diced

1 celery stalk, chopped

3 garlic cloves, minced

1/2 teaspoon turmeric

1 teaspoon paprika

1 tablespoon Cajun spices

1/2 cup unbleached all-purpose flour

6 cups water, vegetable stock or chicken stock

1 (10-oz.) can whole tomatoes, drained and mashed

For best flavor, prepare one day ahead and allow the flavor to develop in the refrigerator. Heat oil in a large pan. Add onion and celery and sauté until onion is almost translucent. Add garlic, then stir in the turmeric, paprika, Cajun spices, and flour. Cook 1 minute, stirring constantly. The mixture will be like a paste. Whisk in the water or stock and reduce heat to lowest setting. Add tomatoes and simmer 15 minutes, stirring often from the bottom to prevent the flour from settling and sticking. Add orzo, beans, and spinach. Cook 5 minutes. Salt to taste. Stir in parsley, lemon peel, and Worcestershire sauce.

YIELD 6 servings

1 serving = 1 vegetable, 2 starches and 2 fats

1/2 cup cooked orzo, pastina pasta, or rice

1 (15-oz.) can garbanzo beans, drained

1 bunch spinach, well washed and chopped, or 1/2 cup frozen spinach, thawed and drained

Salt to taste

1 tablespoon chopped fresh parsley

1/2 teaspoon grated lemon peel

1 teaspoon Worcestershire sauce

CATHRYN'S CARROT-ROSEMARY BISQUE

3 medium-size carrots, diced

2 shallots, minced

1/2 medium-size onion, cut into chunks

1/2 celery stalk, cut into chunks

3 medium-size potatoes, peeled, cut into chunks

4 large carrots, cut into chunks

2 quarts water

1 tablespoon finely chopped fresh rosemary

Salt and white pepper

Place the diced carrots in a medium-size saucepan, cover with water, and simmer until carrots are tender. Reserve carrots and cooking liquid separately. Combine vegetables and the 2 quarts water in pot. Simmer 20 minutes or until carrots are soft. Add rosemary. Cool 1/2 hour. Transfer 2 cups at a time into a blender and purée until smooth. Continue until all is puréed. Transfer back to pot. Add drained cooked carrots and enough cooking liquid to give a creamy consistency. Salt and pepper to taste.

YIELD 6 servings

1 serving = 2 vegetables and 1 starch

SIERRA TORTILLA SOUP

4 chicken thighs
(may remove skin
for less fat)

1/2 onion

1 celery stalk, cut in
half

1 carrot, cut in half

2 garlic cloves,
unpeeled

12 blue corn tortillas

1/4 cup vegetable oil

1/2 onion, diced

6 garlic cloves,
sliced

1/2 cup unbleached
all-purpose flour

1 (10-oz.) can red
chili or red
enchilada sauce

Place chicken, the 1/2 onion, celery, carrot, and the 2 garlic cloves in a large pot. Cover with water and bring to a boil. Reduce heat and simmer 40 minutes or until chicken is tender. Drain through a colander into a large pot, saving the stock. Remove meat from bones and tear into large strips. Reserve stock and chicken meat. Cut tortillas into 1/2″ strips and spray with nonstick cooking spray. Place on a baking sheet and bake in a 400°F oven 5 to 10 minutes or until crispy. Reserve. Add oil and diced onion to a large pot over medium heat. Sauté onion in oil until almost translucent, then add sliced garlic and sauté 1 minute. Stir flour into vegetables and cook 2 minutes, stirring constantly. Add to flour mixture 6 cups of the reserved stock and the red chili sauce. Whisk to combine. Simmer 15 to 20 minutes, stirring constantly. Stir in hominy, beans,

1 (10-oz.) can
golden hominy,
drained

1 (10-oz.) can
pinto beans,
drained

2 green onions,
diced

1/2 bunch cilantro,
stems removed
and leaves
chopped

1 cup shredded
lowfat Monterey
Jack cheese
(4-oz.)

green onions, and cilantro. Add
reserved chicken. Salt to taste. Return
to a simmer and serve in wide bowls
garnished with cheese and tortilla
strips or chips.

YIELD
6 servings
1 serving = 2 proteins, 3 starches, and
2 fats

VARIATIONS
For a vegetarian version of this soup,
eliminate the chicken stock and meat
and substitute water or vegetable
stock.
Blue corn chips can be used in place
of baked tortilla strips for faster
preparation.

HINT
Cool any remaining chicken stock
and refrigerate. Use within three to
four days or freeze for longer storage.

$\mathcal{S}$ONORAN CORN CHOWDER

1/4 cup margarine

1/2 medium-size onion, minced

1 large red bell pepper, diced

1 medium-size jalapeño chile pepper, seeded and minced

1/2 celery stalk, diced

1/2 cup unbleached all-purpose flour

1 teaspoon dried leaf thyme

1/8 teaspoon turmeric

6 cups skim milk

2 cups frozen whole-kernel yellow corn, thawed

1 (10-oz.) can white hominy, drained

1 large potato, cooked and diced

Salt and white pepper to taste

Hot pepper sauce to taste

Canned prickly-pear cactus leaves, cut into strips

Melt margarine in a large pan over medium heat. Add onion, bell pepper, jalapeño, and celery, and sauté until onion is transparent. Add flour, thyme, and turmeric to the vegetables and cook, stirring constantly, 3 minutes. Stir in milk. Bring to a simmer, stirring constantly. Stir in corn, hominy, and potato and return soup to a simmer. Add salt and white pepper to taste. Ladle into bowls and top with a dash of hot pepper sauce and garnish with cactus.

YIELD 8 servings

1 serving = 1 milk, 1 starch, and 1 fat

VARIATION

For a different flavor, buy corn on the cob, and roast it 7 to 10 minutes over an open flame. Cool and cut from the cob. Substitute for the frozen corn.

OLD PUEBLO POTATO BISQUE

1/2 small onion, cut into chunks

1/4 celery stalk, cut into chunks

3 medium-size russet potatoes, peeled and cut into chunks

1 tablespoon dried leaf summer savory

2 bay leaves

2 garlic cloves

2 quarts water or very light vegetable stock

2 cups reduced-fat cream cheese (16 oz.)

1 (4-oz.) can diced green chiles or 2 Anaheim chiles, roasted, peeled, seeded, and diced (page 150)

Salt and pepper to taste

Paprika and finely chopped parsley (to garnish)

Spray large pot with nonstick cooking spray. Combine onion, celery, potatoes, savory, bay leaves, and garlic in a large pot, and cook 5 minutes, stirring constantly. Pour the water or stock over vegetables and bring to a boil. Reduce heat and simmer 15 to 20 minutes or until potatoes are very soft. Cool 1/2 hour. Remove bay leaves from soup. Purée 2 cups soup mixture with 1/3 of the cream cheese and chiles in a blender. Continue processing until all of the soup is puréed. Pour back into pot and bring to a simmer. Season with salt and pepper to taste. Ladle into bowls and sprinkle with paprika and parsley.

YIELD 8 servings

1 serving = 1 vegetable, 1 starch, and 1 fat

COLD FRUIT BISQUE

Purée fruit in a blender or food processor fitted with the metal blade. Fruits like raspberries or blackberries with small seeds should be strained after being puréed. Transfer to a medium-size bowl and stir in yogurt or milk and fructose. Ladle into bowls.

3 cups fresh or frozen fruit (1-1/2 cups thawed or mashed)

1 cup plain nonfat yogurt or skim milk

2 tablespoons granulated fructose

YIELD 4 (1-cup) servings
1 serving = 2 fruits

VARIATIONS

Strawberry & Orange Bisque: Add 1/4 cup orange juice concentrate with the yogurt or milk.

Apple Bisque: Add 1 cup apple-sauce with the yogurt or milk.

HINT

Canned fruits like pineapple, peaches or pears work very well. Use a brand that packs the fruit in natural juice and does not add extra sugar. Use some of the juices to sweeten the bisque instead of the fructose.

CREAM CHEESE & PESTO TORTA

3 cups (1-1/2 lbs.)
reduced-fat
cream cheese
1 cup unsalted butter
1 recipe Pesto
(page 152)
Tomato roses
(see below)
Fresh basil leaves

Soften cream cheese and butter. Beat together until whipped and free of lumps. Line a 1-quart bowl, a small rectangular casserole dish or a 1-quart mold with 3 layers of damp cheesecloth (allow excess for over-hang). Make a 1-1/2-inch-thick layer of the cheese mixture on the bottom of the lined mold. Tap down by gently rapping mold on the countertop. Smooth top with back of a wet spoon. Add a 1/4-inch layer of the Pesto and smooth it over the cheese mixture. Add another layer of the cheese mixture. Tap down. Add another layer of Pesto and spread over cheese mixture. Add a final layer of the cheese mixture. Fold overhanging cheesecloth over top layer and refrigerate at least 4 hours. Fold back cheesecloth and turn mold onto a platter. Gently peel away cheesecloth. Garnish mold with tomato roses and fresh basil leaves. Serve with crackers, sliced baguettes, or rye crisps.

YIELD 6 cups or 96 (1-tablespoon)
servings

1 serving (1-tablespoon) = 1 fat

HINT

To make a Tomato Rose: Peel a con-
tinuous 1/2-inch-wide strip of skin
from tomato, beginning at the stem
end. Use a gentle, sawing motion.
To shape the rose, lay the strip
upside down on a work surface.
Begin rolling at the blossom end of
the strip. If strip breaks just overlap
ends and continue rolling.

Salads & Dressings

RASPBERRY VINAIGRETTE

Combine all ingredients except oil in a blender and purée on high speed 30 seconds. Reduce speed to medium and slowly add the oil in a thin stream. Blend 10 more seconds. Refrigerate in a tightly sealed container for no longer than 7 days.

YIELD   2-1/2 cups or 40 (1-tablespoon) servings
1 serving = 1 fat

1 cup fresh or frozen raspberries (1/2 cup if thawed or mashed)

1 egg yolk (See Note, page 38)

2 tablespoons apple juice

1/4 cup apple cider vinegar

1/2 teaspoon salt (optional)

1/4 teaspoon each dried oregano, marjoram, thyme, basil, ground white pepper, and granulated garlic

1 cup vegetable oil

ASIAN BLEND
DRESSING

Combine all ingredients in a blender and purée on high speed 30 seconds. Store in a tightly sealed container. Use as a salad dressing or serve with raw or slightly steamed vegetables as an appetizer or snack. Refrigerate for no longer than 7 days.

1/2 cup nonfat
cottage cheese

3/4 teaspoon peeled
and minced
ginger root or 1/4
teaspoon ground
ginger

1 tablespoon
chopped fresh
cilantro

2 tablespoons rice
vinegar

1 teaspoon sesame
oil

3/4 cup skim milk

YIELD 1-1/2 cups or 24 (1-tablespoon) servings

1 serving = free exchange

THAI PEANUT DRESSING

Combine coconut milk, peanut butter, tamari or soy sauce, lemon juice, garlic, cayenne, and honey, if using, in a small heavy saucepan and simmer over medium heat 10 minutes. Pour into a blender, add the water and blend on high speed 15 seconds. Add the skim milk and blend again until the mixture is thickened. Refrigerate in a tightly sealed container for no longer than 7 days. Serve as a sauce over Asian Marinated Chicken (page 52) or toss with one of the Oriental noodles such as Chinese Spaghetti, Udon, or Buckwheat Soba noodles cooked al dente. This also makes a good dip for raw or lightly steamed vegetables as an appetizer.

YIELD 1-1/2 cups or 24 (1-tablespoon) servings

1 serving = free exchange

1/2 cup coconut milk

1/4 cup crunchy peanut butter

1-1/2 teaspoons tamari or soy sauce

1 tablespoon fresh lemon juice

1 teaspoon minced garlic

Dash of red (cayenne) pepper

1-1/2 teaspoons honey (optional)

1/3 cup water

1 tablespoon evaporated skim milk

CREAMY ITALIAN DRESSING (NON-DAIRY)

Combine all ingredients in a blender and blend on high speed 30 seconds. Refrigerate in a tightly sealed container for no longer than 10 days; shake before using.

YIELD about 2 cups or 32 (1-table-spoon) servings

1 serving = 2 fats

1/2 cup apple cider vinegar

1-1/3 cups vegetable oil

2 tablespoons fresh lemon juice

3 tablespoons honey

1/2 teaspoon kosher salt

1 teaspoon dried leaf oregano

1/2 teaspoon granulated garlic

1/2 teaspoon dill weed

1/2 teaspoon dried leaf basil

1/4 teaspoon ground black pepper

CREAMY CUCUMBER-DILL DRESSING

Peel, deseed, and grate cucumber; drain off and discard excess liquid. Combine all ingredients in a small bowl and whisk until blended. Refrigerate in a tightly sealed container for no longer than 7 days.

YIELD 2 cups or 32 (1-tablespoon) servings

1 serving = free exchange

HINT

Deseeding a cucumber is easy. Split it in half lengthwise and scrape the seeds out with a small spoon.

1 medium-size cucumber

1 cup plain nonfat yogurt

1/2 cup light sour cream

1 tablespoon chopped fresh dill

1/2 teaspoon cracked pepper

CREAMY TOFU DRESSING

Combine all ingredients in a blender. Purée on high speed 30 seconds or until smooth. Refrigerate no longer than 10 days.

YIELD   1 cup or 16 (1-tablespoon) servings

1 serving = free exchange

4 ounces firm tofu

5 teaspoons balsamic vinegar

2 teaspoons minced garlic

1/2 teaspoon Dijon-style mustard

1/4 cup water

2 tablespoons minced fresh tarragon, basil, or dill

1/2 teaspoon salt

1/4 teaspoon pepper

EASY BLUE-CHEESE DRESSING

Combine all ingredients in a small bowl and whisk until blended. Refrigerate in a tightly sealed container no longer than 7 days.

YIELD 1-1/2 cups or 24 (1-tablespoon) servings

1 serving = 2 fats

1 cup mayonnaise

2 tablespoons lowfat buttermilk

1/4 cup crumbled blue cheese or to taste

1 teaspoon fresh lemon juice

1 teaspoon Worcestershire sauce

1/2 teaspoon white pepper

1/2 teaspoon minced garlic

FRED'S TAMARI-LEMON DRESSING

Combine all ingredients in blender and blend on high speed 30 seconds. Refrigerate in a tightly sealed container for no longer than 7 days.

YIELD 4-3/4 cups or 76 (1-tablespoon) servings

1 serving = 1 fat

1-1/3 cups vegetable oil

3/4 cup water

1/3 cup nutritional yeast

1/3 cup fresh lemon juice

2 cups tamari (do not use soy sauce)

Pinch of red (cayenne) pepper

JICAMA SALAD

Combine all ingredients in a medium-size bowl, cover and marinate in the refrigerator several hours.

YIELD 6 (1/2-cup) servings
1 serving = 1 vegetable

HINT
Jicama is a large, brown root vegetable with a creamy white, crisp interior and sweet flavor.

1 small jicama, peeled and grated
Juice of 1 lime
2 tablespoons chopped cilantro
1 carrot, grated
6 radishes, grated
Dash of hot pepper sauce (optional)

KASHI WITH FRUIT

Steam or boil Kashi in water in a medium-size saucepan 30 minutes or until tender. Cool and add diced fruits, raisins, and cashews, if using. Prepare dressing. Toss salad with dressing, cover, and refrigerate until chilled.

Orange Dressing: Combine all ingredients in a small bowl and whisk until blended.

YIELD 4 servings
1 serving with cashews = 2 fruits, 1 starch, and 1 fat
1 serving without cashews = 2 fruits and 1 starch

1 cup Kashi®
1-1/2 cups water
3/4 cup dried apricots, diced
1 medium-size red apple, diced
1/4 cup raisins
1/4 cup roasted cashews, chopped (optional)
Orange Dressing:
1 teaspoon grated orange peel
.1 cup orange juice
1 teaspoon vegetable oil
1 tablespoon apple cider vinegar

MOCK SOUR CREAM

Combine cottage cheese, buttermilk, and lemon juice in a blender and blend on high speed until smooth. Gently mix in chives or green onions. Use with baked potato or with Mexican dishes.

YIELD About 2 cups or 32 (1-table-spoon) servings

1 serving = free exchange

2 cups nonfat or lowfat cottage cheese

2 tablespoons lowfat buttermilk

2 teaspoons fresh lemon juice

2 tablespoons chopped chives or green onions (optional)

TARRAGON DIPPING SAUCE

Heat the dried tarragon, shallot, and vinegar in a small non-aluminum saucepan over low heat until all liquid is absorbed. Cool. Place the egg yolk in a small bowl. Lightly beat egg yolk with lemon juice. Whisk in oil in a slow, steady stream until it forms a mayonnaise. Add the reduced tarragon mixture and the fresh tarragon and briefly mix until blended. Cover and serve immediately at room temperature. Delicious as a sauce for dipping artichokes or a topping for fish. If preparing ahead, refrigerate for no longer than 3 days.

2 teaspoons dried leaf tarragon

1 shallot, minced

4 teaspoons tarragon vinegar

1 egg yolk (see Note below)

1 tablespoon fresh lemon juice

3/4 cup extra-virgin olive oil

2 teaspoons chopped fresh tarragon

YIELD   1 cup or 16 (1-tablespoon) servings

1 serving = 2 fats

NOTE

The USDA recommends cooking eggs rather than using them raw, due to the presence of salmonella bacteria in some eggs. Beaten whole eggs or yolks heated to 160°F in a double boiler over boiling water are considered safe.

Entrees

Poultry

Seafood

Meat

Vegetarian

Poultry

CHICKEN PAPRIKESH

Melt margarine in a medium-size saucepan. Add onion and sauté until softened. Add the 3/4 cup water. Add remaining ingredients except rice or noodles. Cover and simmer over low heat 35 minutes or until chicken is tender. Serve over rice or noodles.

YIELD 4 servings
1 serving = 3 proteins, 1 vegetable, and 1 starch

1 tablespoon margarine

1 cup chopped onion

3/4 cup water

1 pound boned, skinned chicken breasts, cut into pieces

1 (6-oz.) can tomato paste

1 teaspoon pepper

2 tablespoons paprika

1 teaspoon salt

2 cups cooked rice or noodles

GRILLED CHICKEN SANTA FE

1/4 cup fresh lime juice

1/4 cup extra-virgin olive oil

3/4 teaspoon salt

3/4 teaspoon pepper

4 chicken breasts, skin on, boned

1 cup canned whole tomatillos, peeled

1/4 cup evaporated skim milk

1/2 cup strong chicken stock

1 teaspoon cornstarch mixed with 1 tablespoon water (if needed)

Blue Corn Cakes (page 124)

Salsa Fresca (page 146)

Cilantro and lime wedges (to garnish)

Combine lime juice, olive oil, salt, and pepper to make a marinade. Cut a crosshatch pattern in chicken skin. Brush chicken with marinade; set aside. Purée tomatillos in a blender or food processor fitted with the metal blade. Heat puréed tomatillos in a medium-size saucepan and add the evaporated milk. Reduce by one-half. Add chicken stock and reduce by one-half. Add cornstarch mixture if needed to thicken. Reserve sauce. Preheat grill. Grill chicken 6 to 7 minutes on one side, then 3 minutes on the other side or until the chicken is cooked through. Prepare Blue Corn Cakes. Arrange sauce on plate and top with chicken. Arrange corn cakes on plate. Place salsa on top. Garnish with cilantro and lime.

YIELD 4 servings

1 serving = 4 proteins and 1 fat

ITALIAN STUFFED CHICKEN BREASTS

Preheat oven to 350°F. Spray a baking pan with nonstick cooking spray. Lightly pound chicken breasts between sheets of plastic wrap. Place 1/2 cup stuffing in center of each chicken breast. Roll up around filling. Place seam-side down in prepared baking pan. Sprinkle with the olive oil, oregano, garlic powder, salt, and pepper. Bake 10 to 15 minutes or until chicken is lightly browned and no longer pink in center.

Sauce: Bring stock and evaporated milk to a boil in a medium-size saucepan. Reduce by one-half. Add garlic, tamari, salt, and white pepper. Add cornstarch, if needed, to thicken sauce. Serve over chicken.

YIELD 4 servings

1 serving = 5 proteins and 1 starch

VARIATION

Substitute 2 pounds sole fillets for chicken. Prepare as above except bake 5 to 7 minutes or until sole changes from translucent to opaque.

4 chicken breasts halves, skinned, and boned

1 recipe Spinach Stuffing (page 130)

1 teaspoon extra-virgin olive oil

1/2 teaspoon dried leaf oregano

1/2 teaspoon garlic powder

Salt and pepper to taste

Sauce:

2 cups chicken stock

1 cup evaporated skim milk

2 garlic cloves, minced

1 teaspoon tamari

Salt and white pepper to taste

1 teaspoon cornstarch mixed with 1 tablespoon water (if needed)

1 (10- to 12-lb.) turkey, thawed if frozen

1 onion, skin on, roughly chopped

2 celery stalks, rinsed and broken

2 carrots, rinsed and broken

4 whole garlic cloves, skin on

3 bay leaves

1/2 bunch parsley, rinsed

1/4 cup margarine

1/4 cup kosher salt

2 tablespoons white pepper

2 tablespoons garlic powder

4 cups water

1/4 cup skim milk

1/4 cup unbleached all-purpose flour

Preheat oven to 350°F. Remove giblets from turkey and rinse turkey well inside and out. Stuff cavity with onion, celery, carrots, garlic, bay leaves, and parsley. Rub outside of turkey with margarine. Sprinkle salt, pepper, and garlic powder over the skin. Place turkey in a roasting pan on top of a roasting rack. Add 2 cups of the water to bottom of pan. Roast according to time recommended on turkey packaging (about 20 minutes per pound) or until juices run clear when turkey is pierced with a knife. Remove turkey from pan. Transfer pan juices and vegetables into a medium-size saucepan. Add remaining 2 cups water. Bring to a simmer and cook 10 to 15 minutes. Strain through a cheesecloth into a saucepan. Return to a simmer. Serve as au jus on the side or make into a gravy by whisking milk and flour together, then whisking flour mixture into hot liquid and simmering until thickened.

Remove the skin of the turkey before serving.

YIELD 10 to 12 servings

1 serving = 4 proteins

HINT

If using a thermometer to check when turkey is done, insert it in the thickest part of the thigh about 30 minutes before end of roasting time. Thermometer should register 185°F when turkey is done.

SLOW-BAKED MEXICAN CHICKEN

1-1/4 cups orange
  juice
1-1/4 cups
  grapefruit juice
1/2 cup water
1/4 cup fresh lemon
  juice
1/2 cup achiote
  paste (see Note
  below)
1 (4-lb.) chicken, cut
  up, skin removed,
  or 2 pounds
  boneless, skinless
  chicken meat, cut
  into pieces
Green Rice (page
  117), whole-
  wheat tortillas and
  Calabacitas (page
  105) (to serve)

Combine orange juice, grapefruit juice, water, lemon juice, and achiote paste in a blender; process 1 minute. Pour over chicken in a large casserole dish. Cover and refrigerate 24 hours. Preheat oven to 300°F. Remove chicken from refrigerator, cover and bake 3 hours or until chicken is very tender. Remove from oven and let stand uncovered 20 minutes. Skim off any fat from surface. Transfer to a serving dish. Serve with Green Rice, whole-wheat tortillas, and Calabacitas.

YIELD 8 servings
1 serving = 3 proteins

NOTE

Adobo paste can be substituted for achiote paste, or 1/4 cup chili powder may be used. Achiote paste is available at specialty markets.

VARIATIONS

Slow-Baked Mexican Pork: Substitute 2 pounds pork tenderloin, cut into large pieces, for chicken. Follow directions opposite, but bake 4 hours.

Slow-Baked Mexican Beef: Substitute 2 pounds sirloin steak or top round, cut into large cubes, for chicken. Follow directions opposite.

SPINACH & CHILE CASSEROLE

Preheat oven to 400°F. Spray tortillas with nonstick cooking spray. Place on a baking sheet and bake 5 to 10 minutes or until crispy. Turn oven to 375°F. Lightly spray bottom and sides of a 13"x 9"casserole dish with nonstick cooking spray. Combine jalapeño, onion, garlic, leeks, corn, and turkey or beef in a skillet over medium heat. Cook, stirring occasionally, until onion is transparent. Arrange corn mixture in bottom of casserole dish. Arrange tortilla chips over corn mixture. Layer spinach, green chiles, and cheese over tortilla chips. Combine eggs, milk, flour, salt, cilantro, cumin, and hot pepper sauce in a large bowl. Pour mixture over ingredients in casserole dish just to cover. Bake, uncovered, 1 hour or until set in center. Remove from oven and allow casserole to sit 1/2 hour at room temperature before serving. Cut into squares and serve. Good accompaniments are Green Rice (page 117) and Chihuahua Salsa (page 145).

4 corn tortillas, torn

1 jalapeño chile pepper, seeded and diced

1/2 onion, minced

3 garlic cloves, minced

1/2 cup sliced leeks

1/2 cup frozen whole-kernel yellow corn, thawed

1 pound ground turkey or beef

1 (8-oz.) package frozen chopped spinach, thawed and well drained

1/2 cup diced green chiles, drained

2-1/2 cups shredded lowfat Monterey Jack cheese (10 oz.)

6 eggs

2 cups skim milk

1/2 cup unbleached all-purpose flour

Pinch of salt

1/4 cup chopped cilantro

1 teaspoon ground cumin

2 dashes hot pepper sauce

YIELD 8 servings

1 serving = 3 proteins and 2 starches

VARIATION

Substitute tofu or tempeh for turkey
or beef to make a vegetarian entree.

ASIAN MARINATED CHICKEN

1 teaspoon fennel
    seeds
1 teaspoon crushed
    red pepper flakes
1/2 onion, cut into
    chunks
1/2 carrot, cut into
    chunks
1/4 cup white
    vinegar
2 cups pineapple
    juice
2 pounds boneless
    chicken, cut into
    cubes

Combine fennel seeds, pepper flakes, onion, carrot, vinegar, and pineapple juice in a non-aluminum saucepan. Simmer 10 minutes. Cool and pour over chicken in a glass bowl. Cover and marinate in the refrigerate 24 hours. Stir occasionally to distribute marinade. Preheat grill. Drain and skewer chicken and grill 8 to 10 minutes or until cooked through.

YIELD 4 servings

1 serving = 3 to 4 proteins

VARIATION

Substitute 2 pounds of lean beef for chicken.

HINT

To use marinade as a sauce, strain and add 1 tablespoon cornstarch. Heat to a simmer and cook, stirring, until marinade thickens.

CHICKEN SZECHUAN STYLE

Preheat oven to 350°F. Zest orange peel; set aside. Juice orange and reserve 1/2 cup for sauce. Dice chicken. Spray a medium-size nonstick skillet with nonstick cooking spray and place over medium heat. Add chicken. Cook, stirring occasionally, until browned. Add onions, minced ginger root, pepper flakes, and reserved orange juice. Stir in cornstarch mixture. Cook, stirring, until thickened. Add salt or Mrs. Dash and orange peel. Cook on low heat 15 minutes or until chicken is tender.

YIELD 4 servings

1 serving = 4 proteins

Peel and juice of 1 large orange

2 whole boned chicken breasts, skinned

4 green onions, chopped

1 teaspoon minced ginger root

1/2 teaspoon hot red pepper flakes

1-1/2 teaspoons cornstarch mixed with 1 tablespoon soy sauce

1/2 teaspoon salt or Mrs. Dash®

TEA-POACHED CHICKEN

2 cups juice (apple, orange, or pineapple)

2 orange-and-spice tea bags

2 boned chicken breasts, skinned

1 tablespoon cornstarch mixed with 2 tablespoons water

1 tablespoon chopped parsley

1 orange, peeled and sliced

Bring juice and tea bags to a boil in a small skillet. Reduce heat to simmer. Place chicken breasts in juice and poach (cook) 4 minutes on each side or until cooked through and no longer pink in center. Remove and discard tea bags. Remove chicken from poaching liquid. Reserve on platter. Reduce liquid slightly. Thicken with cornstarch and pour over chicken. Garnish with chopped parsley and orange slices.

YIELD 2 servings

1 serving = 3 to 4 proteins

HINT

Reduce liquid by allowing to simmer uncovered until amount decreases. This intensifies the flavor and thickens the liquid.

RASPBERRY CHICKEN

Heat nonstick cooking spray in a large skillet over medium-high heat. Add chicken and brown lightly, about 3 minutes per side. Remove chicken from skillet and reserve. Meanwhile, press raspberries through a fine strainer to remove the seeds. If holes are too large, first line strainer with cheesecloth. Whisk together cornstarch, stock, vinegar, and raspberry purée in the skillet. Cook over medium heat until mixture begins to thicken. Slowly whisk in milk. Reduce heat to simmer. Add chicken to the sauce and cook, covered, 15 minutes or until chicken is cooked through. Garnish with raspberries and a mint leaf.

2 pounds boned, skinned chicken breast halves

1/2 cup fresh or frozen raspberries

1 tablespoon cornstarch

1/4 cup chicken stock

1/4 cup apple cider vinegar or raspberry vinegar

1/4 cup skim milk

Additional raspberries and mint (for garnish)

YIELD 4 servings

1 serving = 3 proteins

TARRAGON CHICKEN STEW

Bring chicken, broth, carrots, tarragon, pepper, and bay leaf to a boil in a 12-inch skillet or dutch oven. Reduce heat to low. Cover and simmer 30 minutes. Add mushrooms, celery, and onion; bring to a boil. Reduce heat, cover, and simmer until vegetables are soft, about 15 minutes. Discard bay leaf. Stir in apple juice and vinegar and serve.

YIELD 6 (5-oz.) servings

1 serving = 5 proteins and 1 vegetable

2-1/2 pounds boned, skinned chicken breasts, cut into strips

1 cup chicken broth

3 medium-size carrots, chopped

1 tablespoon chopped fresh tarragon or 1 teaspoon dried leaf tarragon

1/8 teaspoon ground pepper

1 bay leaf

1 cup sliced mushrooms

1 celery stalk, chopped

1 medium-size onion, sliced

1/2 cup apple juice

2 tablespoons tarragon vinegar

Seafood

Fish Cakes 59

Fish Puttanesca 60

Gravlox 61

Salmon Croquettes 62

Scallops with Buttered Crumbs 63

Seafood Jambalaya 64

Calamari with Spinach & Oregano 65

Fiesta Fish 66

Marinated Shark 67

Sonoran Seafood Stew 68

Spicy Grilled Catfish 69

FISH CAKES

Spray a nonstick baking sheet with nonstick cooking spray. Combine salmon, perch, shark, and crab in a medium-size bowl. Mix eggs, mayonnaise, mustard, Worcestershire sauce, parsley, onion, crumbs, and seasonings in a small bowl, and add to the seafood mixture. Form into 2-ounce patties and refrigerate 1 hour. Preheat oven to 350°F. Place patties on prepared pan. Bake 15 to 18 minutes or until set and lightly browned. Garnish with capers. Serve with lemon wedges.

YIELD 4 servings

1 serving = 4 proteins

1/4 pound salmon, chopped
1/4 pound perch, chopped
1/4 pound shark, chopped
1/4 pound imitation crab
1 egg, slightly beaten
2 tablespoons light mayonnaise
1 tablespoon Dijon-style mustard

1/2 teaspoon Worcestershire sauce
1 tablespoon chopped fresh parsley
1 tablespoon chopped green onion
1 cup cracker crumbs or soft bread crumbs
Salt, white pepper, and red (cayenne) pepper to taste
Capers (to garnish)
Lemon wedges (to serve)

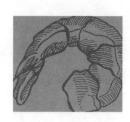

FISH PUTTANESCA

Heat olive oil in a large saucepan. Add onion and garlic and cook until softened. Stir in basil, oregano, and pepper flakes. Add remaining ingredients and simmer 5 minutes or until fish changes from translucent to opaque. Adjust seasonings to taste. Serve over pasta, rice, or Orzo Risotto (page 119).

YIELD 4 servings

1 serving = 3 proteins and 1 vegetable

1 teaspoon extra-virgin olive oil

1 medium-size onion, diced

2 garlic cloves, minced

1 teaspoon dried leaf basil

1 teaspoon dried leaf oregano

1/2 teaspoon crushed red pepper flakes

1 cup water or canned low-sodium clam juice

1 (8-oz.) can Roma (plum) tomatoes, mashed

1/2 cup Niçoise olives or pitted ripe olives

1 tablespoon chopped anchovy

1 tablespoon capers

1 pound fresh firm-fleshed fish (shark, mahi mahi, tuna, monkfish), cubed, or shellfish (shrimp, scallops, or clams)

GRAVLOX

Brush salmon with lemon juice, and oil. Place on a sheet of plastic wrap. Pack remaining ingredients on flesh of salmon. Wrap tightly in plastic wrap. Set on a tray. Place a plate with a 1- or 2-pound can or other weight on top of salmon. Refrigerate 4 to 5 days, turning the salmon from one side to the other every day. Unwrap, scrape off marinade, and slice salmon paper thin on the diagonal. Serve with toasted bagels, cream cheese, capers, red onion, and lemon wedges.

YIELD 4 servings
1 serving = 4 proteins

1 pound fresh salmon fillet (leave skin on)

1 tablespoon lemon juice

1 teaspoon extra-virgin olive oil

2 tablespoons granulated fructose

1 teaspoon kosher salt

1/2 teaspoon white pepper

2 dill sprigs

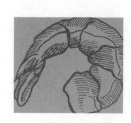

$\mathcal{S}$ALMON CROQUETTES

Preheat oven to 350°F. Spray a baking sheet with nonstick cooking spray. Combine all ingredients in a large bowl, and mix well. Form into 4 patties and place on prepared baking sheet. Bake 20 to 25 minutes or until nicely browned. Garnish with tomato slice, lemon slice, and dill.

YIELD 4 (4-oz.) servings

1 serving = 3 proteins

1 (16-oz.) can salmon, large bones removed

1/4 cup rolled oats

1/4 cup chopped onion

2 tablespoons minced fresh parsley

1/2 teaspoon dill weed

1 teaspoon fresh lemon juice

Dash of salt and pepper (optional) or Mrs. Dash®

1 egg, beaten

Tomato slice, lemon slice and a dill sprig (to garnish)

SCALLOPS WITH BUTTERED CRUMBS

Preheat oven to 400°F. Heat the 1 teaspoon margarine in a medium-size skillet and add carrot and leek. Cook until wilted. Spread on bottom of a 9-inch-square casserole dish. Heat clam juice in a medium-size saucepan to a simmer. Add green onion and milk. Reduce liquid by 1/2. Add scallops. Simmer 3 minutes. Transfer to vegetable-lined casserole dish. Toss bread crumbs with melted margarine, garlic powder and tarragon in a medium-size bowl. Sprinkle on top of scallops. Bake 5 to 10 minutes or until crumbs are golden. Sprinkle with chopped parsley.

YIELD 4 servings

1 serving = 3 proteins, 1 starch, and 1 fat

VARIATION

Substitute 1 cup fish stock made from cubes or packets for clam juice.

1 teaspoon margarine

1 carrot, shredded

1/2 leek, sliced

1 cup canned low-sodium clam juice

1 green onion, minced

1 cup evaporated skim milk

1 pound fresh bay or sea scallops

2 cups bread crumbs (packaged stuffing style)

1 tablespoon margarine, melted

1 teaspoon garlic powder

1 tablespoon dried leaf tarragon

Chopped fresh parsley

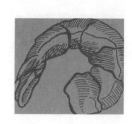

SEAFOOD JAMBALAYA

3 tablespoons margarine

2 tablespoons all-purpose flour

1-1/2 cups chopped onion

1/2 cup chopped bell pepper

1 cup chopped celery

1 garlic clove, minced

Red (cayenne) pepper, to taste

1 (15-oz.) can whole tomatoes

1-1/2 pounds uncooked, peeled shrimp

1 pound crabmeat

2-1/2 cups water

2 cups uncooked white rice

1 (8-oz.) can tomato sauce

Salt to taste

Minced parsley and green onion tops (to garnish)

Heat margarine in a large heavy saucepan, add flour, and cook slowly until golden-brown, stirring constantly. Add onion, bell pepper, celery, garlic, and cayenne. Cook slowly until onion is transparent, stirring often. Add tomatoes and cook until oil rises to the surface. Stir in shrimp, crabmeat, water, rice, and tomato sauce. Cook, covered, over low heat until rice is tender, about 1 hour. Season to taste with salt. Serve hot. Garnish with parsley and green onions.

YIELD 10 servings

1 serving = 3 proteins, 1 starch, and 1 vegetable

VARIATION

Any combination of seafood may be used according to availability.

CALAMARI WITH SPINACH & OREGANO

Heat 1 cup fish stock in a large skillet over medium heat. Add calamari and poach for 5 minutes. Add garlic and cook 3 minutes. Add bell pepper, grape juice, fish stock or water, and tomato sauce. Simmer 10 minutes. Add oregano and simmer 30 minutes more. Add spinach, salt, and black pepper and simmer 2 minutes or until wilted. Serve over angel hair pasta.

YIELD 4 servings

1 serving = 2 proteins and 1 vegetable (without pasta)

1 cup fish stock or clam juice

1 pound cleaned calamari (squid), cut into rings

1 teaspoon minced garlic

1 red bell pepper, diced

3 tablespoons grape juice

3 tablespoons fish stock or water

1 (8-oz.) can tomato sauce

1-1/2 tablespoons chopped fresh oregano

1 (10-oz.) package cleaned spinach leaves

1/2 teaspoon kosher salt

1/2 teaspoon ground black pepper

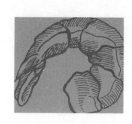

FIESTA FISH

3 tablespoons fresh lemon juice

1 tablespoon chopped fresh basil or 1 teaspoon dried leaf basil

1/2 teaspoon black pepper

1/4 teaspoon chili powder

1 green bell pepper, chopped

1 cup chopped tomatoes

2 tablespoons chopped red onion

1 pound white fish fillets, such as shark or sole

Preheat oven to 350°F. Mix lemon juice, basil, black pepper, and chili powder in a small bowl; set aside. Spray a large nonstick skillet with nonstick cooking spray. Place over medium heat. Add bell pepper, tomatoes, and onion; cook 1 to 2 minutes to soften. Set aside. Place fish in a baking dish. Cover with vegetable mixture. Pour lemon juice mixture over vegetables and fish. Cover dish with foil and bake 20 to 30 minutes or until fish turns from translucent to opaque when tested with a fork.

YIELD 4 (3-oz.) servings

1 serving = 3 proteins

MARINATED SHARK

Cut shark into 4 portions; arrange in a shallow dish. Whisk together the vinegar, olive oil, parsley, and basil in a small bowl and pour over shark. Cover and refrigerate 45 minutes. Preheat grill. Drain off and discard marinade. Grill shark until flesh changes from translucent to opaque. Top each serving with 1 tablespoon of Tomato Vinaigrette.

YIELD 4 servings

1 serving = 4 proteins

1 pound shark (Black Tip/ Mako/Thresher)

1/4 cup balsamic vinegar

2 tablespoons extra-virgin olive oil

1 tablespoon chopped fresh parsley

2 tablespoons chopped fresh basil

4 tablespoons Tomato Vinaigrette (page 154)

Wash mussels and remove beards. Place cornmeal in enough salted water to cover the mussels and soak for half a day. Drain and discard any mussels that do not close when tapped. Wash clams, discarding any that remain open. Peel shrimp, removing tails. Cut fish into cubes. Heat olive oil in a medium-size saucepan over medium heat. Add onion and garlic; cook until softened. Add tomatoes, green chiles, orange juice and peel, oregano, and clam juice or fish stock. Simmer 10 minutes. Add fish and spice paste. Simmer 10 minutes. Discard shellfish that do not open. Serve in flat soup bowls over rice or Orzo Risotto. Garnish with lime wedges and tortilla strips.

10 mussels

1 tablespoon cornmeal

5 clams

1/4 pound shrimp

1/2 pound assorted firm-fleshed fish

1 teaspoon extra-virgin olive oil

1/2 cup diced onion

1 garlic clove, chopped

1 (8-oz.) can diced tomatoes

1 (6-oz.) can diced green chiles

Peel and juice of 1 orange

1/2 tablespoon chopped fresh oregano

1 (10-oz.) bottle clam juice or 1-1/4 cups good fish stock

Paste made with 1 teaspoon ground cumin, 1 teaspoon chili powder, and 1 tablespoon water

Cooked rice or Orzo Risotto (page 119) (to serve)

Lime wedges and blue corn tortilla strips (to garnish)

YIELD 5 servings

1 serving = 4 proteins and 1 vegetable (without rice or Orzo Risotto)

HINT

For salted water, use 1/3 cup salt to 1 gallon of water.

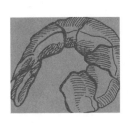

 PICY GRILLED
CATFISH

Arrange catfish fillets in a shallow dish. Combine lemon juice, soy sauce, vegetable oil, ginger root, garlic, onions, paprika, and cayenne in a small bowl or jar. Pour over catfish. Cover and marinate in the refrigerator 1 to 2 hours. Remove catfish from marinade. Preheat grill or broiler. Grill or broil 4 minutes on each side or until catfish turns from translucent to opaque when tested with a fork. Serve with roasted red potatoes.

YIELD 4 servings

1 serving = 4 proteins

4 catfish fillets (6-oz. each)

1/4 cup fresh lemon juice

1/4 cup soy sauce

1 teaspoon vegetable oil

2 tablespoons finely chopped ginger root or 2 teaspoons ground ginger

6 garlic cloves, finely chopped or minced (1 tablespoon)

3 green onions, chopped

2 tablespoons minced onion

1 teaspoon paprika

1/4 or 1/2 teaspoon red (cayenne) pepper

Meat

Hungarian Beef &
Caraway Goulash 73

Leon's Mexican Beef Stew 74

Roast Beef 75

Sierra's Famous Marinated Steak 77

Mustard-Crusted Baked Ham 78

Pork Tenderloin Medallions 79

Sierra BBQ Ribs 80

Turkish Stuffed Tomatoes 81

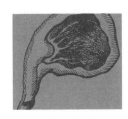

HUNGARIAN BEEF & CARAWAY GOULASH

Heat oil in a medium-size saucepan. Add beef and cook until brown. Add onion, garlic, marjoram, cumin, caraway seeds, and paprika. Cook 10 minutes, stirring occasionally. Add bell peppers, beef stock, and tomato paste. Cover and simmer 1-1/2 hours, stirring often. Add more stock if liquid reduces too much. Remove from heat. Stir in yogurt, salt, and pepper. Serve over cooked egg noodles or spinach noodles.

YIELD 4 servings

1 serving = 3 proteins and 1 vegetable

1 teaspoon extra-virgin olive oil

1 pound beef for stew, cubed

1 medium-size onion, diced

4 garlic cloves, minced

1 tablespoon ground marjoram

1/2 tablespoon ground cumin

1 tablespoon caraway seeds (crushed slightly with back of spoon)

1 tablespoon Hungarian paprika

1/2 red bell pepper, diced

1/2 green bell pepper, diced

1 cup beef stock

1 (6-oz.) can tomato paste

8 ounces nonfat yogurt

Salt and pepper to taste

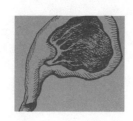

$\mathcal{L}$EON'S MEXICAN BEEF STEW

Combine all ingredients in a large saucepan and bring to a simmer. Cook over low heat about 1 hour or until the liquid evaporates, being careful not to burn. Serve with rice, beans and flour tortillas.

**1 pound beef brisket,
or top round
cooked and
shredded
(trim off fat)**

**1 (4-oz.) can diced
green chiles**

**1/2 large onion,
chopped**

**1 (15-oz.) can diced
tomatoes**

**2 garlic cloves,
crushed**

**1/2 green bell
pepper, chopped**

**1/4 teaspoon ground
cinnamon**

1 tablespoon vinegar

**1 jalapeño chile
pepper, minced**

YIELD 4 servings

1 serving = 3 proteins and 1 vegetable

HINT

To cook the meat, boil brisket in water for 2 to 3 hours, drain, cool, and shred. For top round—roast until well done (40 minutes/pound), cool, and shred with grain of meat.

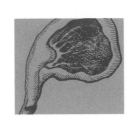

ROAST BEEF

Preheat oven to 350°F. Place onion, celery, carrots, garlic, bay leaves, and parsley in bottom of a roasting pan. Rub roast with salt, pepper, and garlic powder. Place on top of vegetables and add 2 cups of the water to pan. Roast 20 minutes per pound for medium (11 to 12 minutes per pound longer for well-done meat). Remove roast from pan and let sit 10 to 15 minutes before carving. Trim fat from outside of roast before serving. Transfer pan juices and vegetables to a medium-size saucepan. Add remaining 2 cups water. Bring to a simmer and cook 10 to 15 minutes. Strain through a cheesecloth into a saucepan. Return to a simmer. Combine cornstarch and the 3 tablespoons water. Whisk into pan juices. Let simmer, whisking, until thickened. Serve as a gravy.

1 onion, skin on, roughly chopped

2 celery stalks, rinsed and broken

2 carrots, rinsed and broken

4 whole garlic cloves, skin on

3 bay leaves

1/2 bunch fresh parsley, rinsed

1 (2- to 3-lb.) beef roast (top round, standing rib, or rib eye)

1/4 cup kosher salt

2 tablespoons white pepper

2 tablespoons garlic powder

4 cups water

3 tablespoons cornstarch

3 tablespoons cold water

YIELD 7 servings

1 serving = 4 proteins

HINT

Temperatures for degrees of doneness are as follows: rare (140°F),
medium (150°F) and well done
(170°F). Remove roast from oven
when the internal temperature is
about 5 degrees less than the desired
temperature. Cover with foil and let
stand 10 to 15 minutes. The temperature will rise about 5 degrees while
standing.

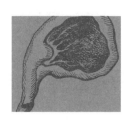

$\mathscr{S}$ IERRA'S FAMOUS MARINATED STEAK

Coarsely chop ginger root, celery, and onion. Add all ingredients except steak to a large saucepan. Bring to a simmer and remove from heat. Do not boil. Refrigerate overnight. Place meat in a shallow container. Strain mixture and pour over meat. Marinate 5 to 6 hours. Preheat grill. Drain meat and discard marinade. Grill meat to desired doneness.

YIELD 4 servings

1 serving = 3 to 4 proteins

1 (1-inch) piece
   ginger root

1 celery stalk

1/2 medium-size
   onion

2 garlic cloves

1 cup reduced-
   sodium tamari or
   1/2 cup regular
   soy sauce

1 cup fresh lemon
   juice

1 cup water

2 pounds top sirloin
   beef steak

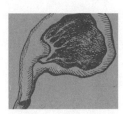

MUSTARD-CRUSTED BAKED HAM

Preheat oven to 300°F. Mix mustard with Worcestershire sauce. Rub ham with mixture. Combine bread crumbs with parsley. Roll ham in crumbs. Place on rack in a baking pan and bake 1 to 1-1/2 hours or until crumbs are golden and ham is juicy and hot. Let ham sit 10 to 15 minutes before carving.

1 (12-oz.) jar Dijon-style mustard

1/4 cup Worcestershire sauce

1 (6- to 8-lb.) boneless ham shank

6 cups Japanese bread crumbs

1/4 cup dried parsley flakes

YIELD 15 to 20 (4-oz.) servings
1 serving = 4 proteins and 1 starch

HINT

If purchasing a smoked ham shank, have the butcher remove the bone (keep it for soup) or purchase a pre-boned ham. Remove packaging and trim off all but 1/8 inch of fat from outside of ham.

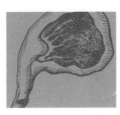

PORK TENDERLOIN MEDALLIONS

Cut tenderloin into 4 medallions, cutting on the diagonal. Mix flour, salt, pepper, and garlic powder in a shallow bowl. Dredge medallions in seasoned flour. Melt margarine in a medium-size skillet over medium heat. Add medallions and cook, turning once, until no longer pink in center. Deglaze the pan with beef stock. Remove medallions to a warm platter. Add evaporated milk to pan juices and reduce slightly. Add applesauce. Spoon sauce over pork, garnish, and serve with Potato Pancakes.

YIELD 4 servings

1 serving = 4 proteins and 1 starch

1 (1-lb.) pork tenderloin

1 cup unbleached all-purpose flour

1 tablespoon salt

1 teaspoon white pepper

1 teaspoon garlic powder

1/2 tablespoon margarine

1/4 cup beef stock

1/2 cup evaporated skim milk

2 tablespoons applesauce

Potato Pancakes (page 126)

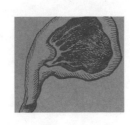

SIERRA BBQ RIBS

6 pounds baby back pork ribs

1 onion, finely diced

1 cup ketchup

1-1/2 cups water

2 tablespoons prepared horseradish

2 tablespoons honey

2 tablespoons Worcestershire sauce

1/4 cup vinegar

1/2 tablespoon salt

2 tablespoons Dijon-style mustard

Large dash hot pepper sauce

1 tablespoon Liquid Smoke

Parboil ribs in a large pan or steam 20 minutes. Preheat oven to 300°F. Combine and refrigerate all ingredients except ribs. Lay ribs out on a large baking sheet and cover with parchment paper or foil. Slow bake ribs 2 hours. Remove cover and drain off fat. Generously cover the ribs with the sauce and return to the oven 20 to 30 minutes or until ribs are crispy and bubbly.

YIELD 6 servings

1 serving = 4 proteins and 1 fat

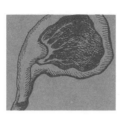 

TURKISH STUFFED TOMATOES

Heat a large skillet; add lamb and garlic. Cook, stirring to break up lamb, until no longer pink. Add cumin, oregano, spinach, and mushrooms. Remove from heat. Drain off any fat. Add couscous, feta cheese, and salt and pepper to taste. Core and hollow tomatoes, leaving a 1/4-inch-thick shell. Preheat broiler. Fill tomatoes with lamb mixture. Place stuffed tomatoes in a broiler pan. Sprinkle with Parmesan cheese. Place about 4 inches from broiler and broil until lightly browned, 10 minutes.

YIELD 6 tomatoes

1 serving = 4 proteins, 1/2 starch, 1 vegetable, and 1 fat (with lamb)

1 serving = 1 protein, 1 starch, and 1 vegetable (without lamb)

1-1/2 pounds ground lamb

1 garlic clove, minced

1 tablespoon ground cumin

1 tablespoon dried leaf oregano

1 cup fresh spinach, chopped

1 cup finely chopped mushrooms

2 cups cooked couscous (page 120)

4 ounces feta cheese, finely crumbled

Salt and pepper to taste

6 large tomatoes

3 tablespoons grated Parmesan cheese

VARIATION

For a vegetarian dish, substitute 2 cups cooked brown rice for lamb. Add with the couscous.

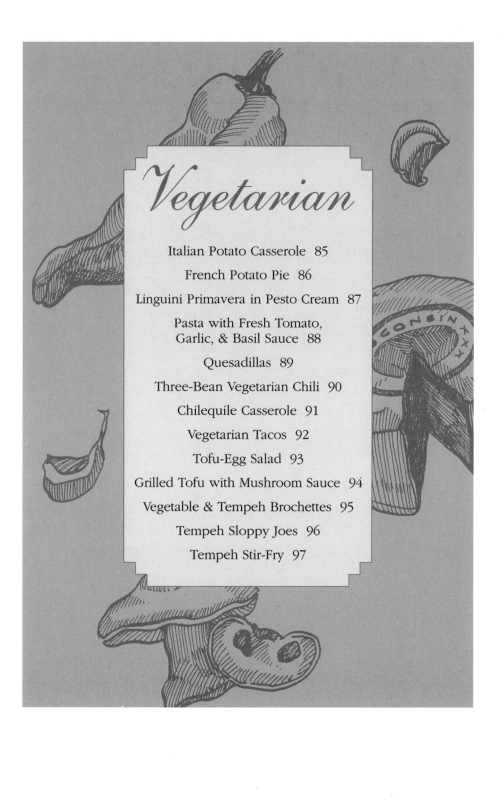

Vegetarian

Italian Potato Casserole 85

French Potato Pie 86

Linguini Primavera in Pesto Cream 87

Pasta with Fresh Tomato,
Garlic, & Basil Sauce 88

Quesadillas 89

Three-Bean Vegetarian Chili 90

Chilequile Casserole 91

Vegetarian Tacos 92

Tofu-Egg Salad 93

Grilled Tofu with Mushroom Sauce 94

Vegetable & Tempeh Brochettes 95

Tempeh Sloppy Joes 96

Tempeh Stir-Fry 97

ITALIAN POTATO CASSEROLE

A day ahead, boil the potatoes in their skin until barely tender. Drain, cool, and refrigerate. The next day, preheat oven to 350°F. Spray a large, shallow casserole dish with nonstick cooking spray. Peel the potatoes and cut into thick slices. Arrange in prepared casserole dish. Slice the tomatoes and place them on top of potatoes and sprinkle with the salt, pepper, and basil. Cut mozzarella cheese into strips and arrange crosswise on the tomatoes. Mix cottage cheese or ricotta cheese with the parsley, salt, and pepper in a small bowl. Spread mixture evenly over mozzarella cheese. Sprinkle top with Parmesan cheese. Bake 30 to 40 minutes or until top is well browned.

YIELD 6 servings

1 serving = 2 proteins, 2 starches, and 1 vegetable

2 pounds russet potatoes

1-1/2 pounds tomatoes

1/2 teaspoon salt

Pepper to taste

2 tablespoons chopped fresh basil

10 ounces part-skim mozzarella cheese

3/4 cup lowfat cottage cheese or part-skim ricotta cheese

2/3 cup chopped fresh parsley

1/2 teaspoon each salt and pepper

1/4 cup grated Parmesan cheese

FRENCH POTATO PIE

1 (9-inch) whole-wheat pie shell (ready made)

26 to 30 ounces russet potatoes, peeled and steamed until soft

2 green onions, minced

2 eggs

1 teaspoon kosher salt

1/2 teaspoon white pepper

1/4 teaspoon grated nutmeg

1/2 cup nonfat cottage cheese

1/2 cup light sour cream or plain nonfat yogurt

2 tablespoons grated Parmesan cheese

Red Pepper Purée (page 150)

Preheat oven to 400°F. Prebake pie shell 3 to 4 minutes or until golden. Reduce oven temperature to 350°F. Mash potatoes with an electric mixer or by hand until very smooth. Place a small nonstick skillet over medium heat. Add onions and cook until transparent. Add to potatoes. Stir in remaining ingredients except Parmesan cheese and pepper purée. Spread potato mixture in baked pie shell. Top with Parmesan cheese. Bake 30 minutes or until golden-brown and mixture is firm. Serve with pepper purée.

YIELD 8 servings

1 serving = 1 protein, 1 starch, and 1 fat

LINGUINI PRIMAVERA IN PESTO CREAM

1/2 cup julienned
carrots

1/2 cup julienned
onion

1/2 cup julienned
zucchini

1/2 cup julienned
red bell pepper

1/2 cup
cauliflowerets

1 cup sliced summer
squash

1/4 cup sliced
mushrooms

1/2 cup julienned
green beans

2 tablespoons Pesto
(page 152)

1/4 cup evaporated
skim milk

1/4 cup grated
Parmesan cheese

1/2 pound linguini,
cooked

Salt, white pepper,
and nutmeg to
taste

Parsley, chopped

Steam all vegetables until crisp-tender, steaming the firmest vegetables about 3 minutes and ending with the mushrooms 30 seconds. Plunge into cold water and reserve. Heat a large skillet, add Pesto and cook 2 minutes. Drain vegetables and stir into Pesto to coat and reheat. Add milk and bring to a simmer. Add cheese and stir until melted. Add cooked linguini and toss all together. Season with salt, white pepper, and nutmeg. Garnish with chopped parsley.

YIELD 4 servings

1 serving = 1 protein, 1 starch, and 1 vegetable

PASTA WITH FRESH TOMATO, GARLIC, & BASIL SAUCE

Combine all ingredients except pasta in a large bowl, cover, and let stand at room temperature 2 hours before serving. Cook pasta according to package directions until tender but firm to the bite. Drain pasta, but do not rinse. Toss pasta with tomato sauce and serve.

1 (15-oz.) can Roma (plum) tomatoes with juice, broken

2 large, ripe tomatoes, diced

8 ounces Feta cheese, crumbled (optional)

1/4 cup fresh basil, cut into strips

4 garlic cloves, minced

1 tablespoon extra-virgin olive oil

Dash of kosher salt

Dash of cracked pepper

8 ounces pasta

YIELD 4 servings

1 serving = 1 starch and 3 vegetables (without Feta)

1 serving = 2 proteins, 1 starch, and 3 vegetables (with Feta)

QUESADILLAS

Heat a large skillet or griddle over medium heat on stovetop or preheat broiler. Sprinkle equal amounts of cheeses, chiles, cilantro, and onion on each tortilla. Place in hot skillet or under broiler. Reduce heat to low and cook until cheeses melt. Fold each tortilla in half. Transfer to a cutting board and cut into 3 wedges. Serve warm with salsa and salad.

YIELD 4 servings

1 serving = 2 proteins, 2 starches, and 1 fat

VARIATION

Add browned ground beef, cooked chicken, or refried beans for a more substantial quesadilla.

1 cup shredded lowfat Monterey Jack cheese (4 oz.)

1 cup shredded lowfat Cheddar cheese (4 oz.)

1/4 cup diced, canned mild green chiles

1/4 cup chopped fresh cilantro

1 green onion, finely minced

4 large whole-wheat flour tortillas

Salsa Fresca (page 146) and Jicama Salad (page 35) (to serve)

THREE-BEAN VEGETARIAN CHILI

1 cup dried Anasazi beans or pinto beans

1 cup dried black beans

1 cup dried white beans or other favorite bean

1/2 medium-size onion, diced

1/2 green bell pepper, diced

1 medium-size jalapeño chile pepper, seeds removed and minced

1 medium-size carrot, diced

2 tomatoes, peeled, seeded, and chopped

4 garlic cloves, minced

1 tablespoon ground cumin

1 tablespoon pasilla chile powder

1 teaspoon dried leaf oregano

1 tablespoon unbleached all-purpose flour

1/4 teaspoon red (cayenne) pepper (optional)

1 (10-oz.) can whole tomatoes, pureed

Salt to taste

Soak beans separately 24 hours in enough water to cover. Pour off water and rinse. Cover with fresh water and bring beans to a boil and boil 10 minutes (in separate pans). Drain off water and add enough fresh water to cover. Continue simmering beans until each becomes tender. Drain and reserve. Heat a large pan. Add onion, green bell pepper, jalapeño, carrot, chopped tomatoes, and garlic. Cook over low heat to extract the natural juices. (This is called "sweating" the vegetables.) Continue cooking until onion is tender, stirring occasionally. Stir in cumin, chile powder, oregano, flour, and cayenne, if using, and cook 1 or 2 minutes. Add canned tomatoes and cooked beans. Simmer 30 minutes. Add salt to taste. This is best when made at least one day ahead and refrigerated to allow flavors to develop.

YIELD 6 servings

1 serving = 2 starches and 1 vegetable

CHILEQUILE CASSEROLE

Preheat oven to 375°F. Lightly oil a 13" x 9" baking dish. Tear 1/2 of the tortillas into bite-size pieces; spread evenly on bottom of baking dish. Layer 1/2 of the green chiles, jalapeños, cheese, tomatoes, garlic, onion, beans, cumin, and oregano over tortillas. Repeat layers beginning with the tortillas, then remaining ingredients. Mix together eggs, buttermilk, salt, and pepper in a medium-size bowl. Slowly pour over casserole. Bake, uncovered, 35 minutes or until eggs are set. Serve hot.

YIELD 10 servings

1 serving = 1 protein and 2 starches

10 corn tortillas

1/2 cup diced green chiles

2 jalapeño chile peppers, diced

1/2 cup shredded lowfat Monterey Jack cheese (2 oz.)

1 cup diced tomatoes

1 or 2 garlic cloves, minced

1/2 cup chopped onion

2 cups mashed cooked pinto beans or refried beans

1 teaspoon ground cumin

1/4 teaspoon dried leaf oregano

3 eggs, slightly beaten

2 cups buttermilk

Dash salt and pepper

Rinse lentils; drain. Combine lentils, onion, bell pepper, and water in a medium-size saucepan. Bring to a boil; reduce heat. Cover and simmer about 30 minutes or until tender and liquid is absorbed. Stir tomato sauce and spices into lentils. Simmer, uncovered, about 5 minutes. Stir in tofu; heat through. Spoon into tortillas. Top with lettuce and tomato.

1/4 cup lentils
1/4 cup chopped onion
1/4 cup chopped green bell pepper
1/2 cup water
1 (8-oz.) can tomato sauce
1 tablespoon chili powder
1/8 teaspoon pepper
8 ounces tofu, drained and finely chopped
8 corn tortillas
1-1/2 cups shredded lettuce
1 medium-size tomato, chopped

YIELD 8 tacos

1 taco = 1 protein and 1 starch

VARIATION

Bulgur Tacos: Prepare as above, except substitute bulgur for lentils. Cover and simmer bulgur, onion, and 3/4 cup water about 10 minutes or until tender and liquid is absorbed.

HINT

Warm tortillas in a microwave or regular oven. Wrap in a damp paper towel if using the microwave oven. Wrap in foil before heating in a regular oven.

TOFU-EGG SALAD

Cut tofu into 1/2-inch cubes and steam in steamer basket 10 minutes. Remove, cool, and drain well. Coarsely chop, then mince bell pepper, onion, celery, and parsley in a food processor fitted with the metal blade. Mix vegetables with mayonnaise, yeast, turmeric, mustard, salt, and pepper in a medium-size bowl. Gently stir in tofu cubes, cover, and refrigerate overnight before serving.

YIELD 6 sandwiches or stuffing for 6 tomatoes
1 serving = 2 proteins, 2 starches, and 1 fat (on bread)
1 serving = 2 proteins, 1 vegetable, and 1 fat (in tomato)

3 (10-oz.) packages tofu, drained
1/2 red bell pepper
1 green onion
1/2 celery stalk
1 parsley sprig
1/2 cup light mayonnaise
1 tablespoon nutritional yeast (page 171)
1/8 teaspoon turmeric
1/2 tablespoon Dijon-style mustard
Salt and pepper to taste

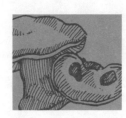

GRILLED TOFU WITH MUSHROOM SAUCE

2 (10-oz.) packages firm tofu, cut into 8 slices

2 cups vegetable stock

1/4 cup tamari or soy sauce

1/2 tablespoon toasted sesame oil

1 cup sliced button mushrooms or shiitake mushrooms

2 garlic cloves, minced

Steam tofu over boiling water 30 to 40 minutes or until heated through and firm. Save steaming water for soup or stock. Mix together vegetable stock and tamari or soy sauce in a small bowl. Place steamed tofu in a shallow bowl; pour stock mixture over tofu. Marinate in the refrigerator 2 to 6 hours. Drain, reserving any liquid for mushroom sauce. To prepare mushroom sauce, heat sesame oil in a medium-size skillet over medium-high heat. Add mushrooms and garlic; cook 3 to 5 minutes or until browned. Add any reserved marinade and reduce heat to low. Cook about 20 minutes or until liquid is reduced by about half. Preheat gas or charcoal grill. Handling carefully, grill tofu as you would meat. (Or bake tofu 25 minutes in a 400°F oven.) Serve topped with mushroom sauce.

YIELD 4 servings

1 serving = 2 proteins

VEGETABLE & TEMPEH BROCHETTES

Clean and trim vegetables, cutting bell peppers and onion into wide wedges. If using a firm vegetable like yam or corn, parboil or steam them first. If using tofu, steam 10 minutes and drain well, or prebake the cubes in an oiled pan 10 minutes in a 350°F oven to firm them. Skewer the vegetables with the tempeh or tofu, alternating according to your choice of color. Marinate 1 hour in Italian dressing or Asian Blend Dressing. Preheat grill. Grill 10 minutes over hot coals, turning 3 times.

YIELD 8 to 10 brochettes

1 serving = 1 protein, 1 starch, and 2 vegetables (tempeh)

1 serving = 1 protein and 1 vegetable (tofu)

16 medium-size mushrooms

1 green bell pepper

1 red bell pepper

1 red onion

2 or 3 of the following: zucchini, eggplant, yellow squash, corn on the cob, or yam, cut into 1/2-inch rounds or cubes

20 ounces tempeh or tofu, cut into 1/2-inch cubes

Italian dressing or Asian Blend Dressing (page 28)

TEMPEH SLOPPY JOES

Cook onion, bell peppers, and tomatoes in their own juices in a large skillet. Stir in garlic, chili powder, cumin, mustard, cayenne, cloves, and cinnamon. Add water, tomato paste, soy sauce, and lemon juice. Bring to a simmer. Add crumbled tempeh and heat thoroughly. Serve over a whole-wheat bun, open faced, with cheese.

YIELD 4 servings

1 serving = 4 proteins, 2 starches, and 2 vegetables (with tempeh)

1 serving = 4 proteins, 2 starches, and 2 vegetables (with beef)

VARIATION

Substitute 1 pound lean ground beef or turkey for the tempeh. Cook meat with the vegetables.

1 cup diced onion

1/2 cup diced red bell pepper

1/2 cup diced green bell pepper

1-1/2 cups chopped tomatoes

2 garlic cloves, minced

1/2 tablespoon chili powder

1/2 tablespoon ground cumin

1 teaspoon dry mustard

Pinch each of red (cayenne) pepper, cloves, and cinnamon

1/2 cup water

1/4 cup tomato paste

1-1/2 tablespoons soy sauce

2 tablespoons fresh lemon juice or lime juice

2 cups crumbled tempeh

4 whole-wheat buns

1 cup shredded lowfat Cheddar cheese (4 oz.)

TEMPEH STIR-FRY

Steam tempeh over boiling water 5 minutes. Chop tempeh into 1-inch cubes and set aside. Heat oils in a large skillet or wok. Add tempeh and water chestnuts; stir-fry 1 minute. Stir in ginger root, garlic, and water. Add carrots, bell peppers, onions, soy sauce, and stir-fry 5 minutes or until vegetables are crisp-tender. Sir in pepper flakes and cilantro.

YIELD 4 servings

1 serving = 4 proteins, 1 starch, 1 fat and 1 vegetable

20 ounces tempeh

1/2 tablespoon vegetable oil

1/2 tablespoon sesame oil

1/2 cup sliced water chestnuts

2 tablespoons minced ginger root

1/2 teaspoon minced garlic

2 teaspoons water

1 cup thinly sliced carrots

1 cup chopped green bell pepper

1 cup chopped red bell pepper

1/2 cup chopped green onions

1/3 cup reduced-sodium soy sauce

Pinch of crushed red pepper flakes

2 tablespoons chopped cilantro

Fruits & Vegetables

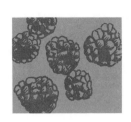

APPLESAUCE

Cook apples, water, cinnamon, and cloves together in a non-aluminum pan with a lid. Stir occasionally and check that apples do not burn. Cook until apples are soft. Remove from heat and let stand awhile. Remove spices. Place apples in a food mill over a bowl and put apples through mill. Stir lemon juice and honey into applesauce to taste. Refrigerate in jars up to 1 week.

YIELD 10 servings

1 serving = 1 fruit

10 cooking apples (Pippin, Empire, Winesap, Jonathan, or Granny Smith), peeled, cored, and sliced

1/2 cup water

1 cinnamon stick

1/4 teaspoon whole cloves

1 tablespoon fresh lemon juice

Honey to taste

BANANA MUSHEE

Combine all ingredients in a large saucepan and cook slowly over low heat 25 to 30 minutes or until heated through, stirring often. Or bake in a casserole dish in a 350°F oven 25 to 30 minutes. Serve hot or cold.

5 ripe bananas,
   sliced
1/4 cup raisins
1/4 cup
   unsweetened
   pineapple juice
1/4 cup
   unsweetened
   pineapple chunks
   (optional)
1/4 teaspoon ground
   cinnamon
1/8 teaspoon each
   ground cloves
   and nutmeg

YIELD 13 (1/4-cup) servings
1 serving = 1 fruit (with pineapple)

BAKED PUMPKIN

Preheat oven to 350°F. Spray a 1-quart glass casserole dish with nonstick cooking spray. Sauté spices in margarine in a small skillet 1 minute to release flavors. Remove from heat. Combine all ingredients in a medium-size bowl and mix. Pour into prepared casserole dish. Bake 30 minutes or until pumpkin is set and browned. Serve with Mustard-Crusted Baked Ham (page 78) or grilled fish.

YIELD 4 to 6 servings

1 serving = 1 starch

1/2 teaspoon ground cinnamon

1 teaspoon garam masala (page 170)

1 tablespoon margarine

2 (10-oz.) cans unsweetened pumpkin

2 eggs, beaten

1/4 cup evaporated skim milk

1 tablespoon granulated fructose

BROCCOLI & ROASTED PEPPERS

1 teaspoon extra-virgin olive oil

3 garlic cloves, minced

1 cup roasted, julienned red bell peppers (see Note below)

4 cups broccoli flowerets, steamed until crisp-tender

2 tablespoons vegetable stock or water

Black pepper

Heat oil in a medium-size saucepan over low heat. Add garlic and cook until garlic turns golden. Do not burn. Stir in roasted peppers and cook briefly. Add steamed broccoli and vegetable broth or water, cover, and cook, stirring every few minutes, until hot. Season with black pepper and serve.

YIELD 4 to 6 servings

1 serving = 1 vegetable

NOTE

Roasted bell peppers are available in jars or roast your own (page 150).

Heat oil in a medium-size saucepan. Add onion and zucchini and cook over medium-high heat until lightly browned. Add the corn, tomatoes, cilantro, salt, and pepper. Reduce heat to medium and cook vegetables 3 to 5 minutes, stirring occasionally. Top with cheese and serve.

YIELD 5 (1/2-cup) servings
1 serving = 1/2 starch, 1 vegetable, and 1 fat

2 tablespoons extra-virgin olive oil

1/2 cup diced red onion

2 cups sliced zucchini

1 cup whole-kernel yellow corn (fresh or frozen)

1 cup diced tomatoes

1/4 cup chopped cilantro

1/2 teaspoon salt

1/4 teaspoon ground white pepper

1/2 cup shredded Cheddar or Monterey Jack Cheese (2 oz.)

GINGERED ACORN SQUASH

2 medium-size acorn
squash

4 tablespoons
unsweetened
orange juice

1 teaspoon ground
ginger

1 teaspoon grated
nutmeg

Preheat oven to 375°F. Halve the squash from stem end to bottom. Remove the seeds and discard. Slice a thin piece off bottom of each half so that the squash will stand straight. Arrange the 4 halves in a shallow baking dish to fit. Add about 1/2 inch water to bottom of dish. Place 1 tablespoon orange juice and 1/4 teaspoon each of the ginger and nutmeg into each squash half. Cover the dish with foil and bake 1 to 1-1/4 hours or until tender. Remove from oven, discard foil, and let rest 5 minutes before serving so that juices can penetrate squash.

YIELD 4 servings

1 serving = 1 starch

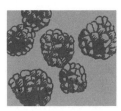

MAQUECHOU (STEWED CORN & TOMATOES)

Cut corn lengthwise off cob. Scrape cob to get juice. Mix all ingredients except oil in a medium-size saucepan. Heat oil and add to vegetables. Cover and simmer about 45 minutes, stirring occasionally, or until vegetables are cooked.

YIELD 8 servings

1 serving = 1 starch

8 ears of corn

1/2 cup chopped onion

1/4 cup chopped bell pepper

1/2 cup peeled, chopped tomato

1 teaspoon granulated fructose

Salt and pepper to taste

1 tablespoon extra-virgin olive oil

ROASTED WINTER VEGETABLES

1 celery stalk
2 red potatoes
4 parsnips
2 turnips
2 rutabagas
3 carrots
2 yams
1 onion
4 garlic cloves
1/2 bunch fresh
 parsley
2 bay leaves
1 teaspoon kosher
 salt
1/2 teaspoon
 cracked black
 pepper

Preheat oven to 375°F. Scrub all vegetables well (peel if necessary). Peel onion and garlic. Chop all vegetables, parsley, and bay leaves into 2-inch pieces (leave garlic whole) and toss with salt and pepper. Place in a 2-inch-deep baking dish. Add about 1/2 inch of water to pan. Cover with foil and bake 20 minutes. Remove foil and continue baking 20 minutes longer or until vegetables are well browned and tender. Serve with roasted meat or with cheese and bread.

YIELD 8 servings

1 serving = 1 starch and 2 vegetables

PAGHETTI SQUASH ITALIAN

Preheat oven to 350°F. Spray a baking sheet with nonstick cooking spray. Cut squash in half lengthwise and remove seeds. Place cut-sides down on prepared baking sheet and bake 30 minutes or until tender. Remove from oven and turn cut-side up to cool. When cool, use a large kitchen spoon to scoop out the inside of the squash, then, with your hands, break fibers into noodle-like strands. Heat olive oil in a medium-size saucepan. Add garlic, bell pepper, mushrooms, and dried herbs; cook, stirring occasionally, until vegetables are wilted. Add the water and bring to a simmer. Season with salt and black pepper. Stir in tomato and olives and pour over squash. Top with chopped parsley. Serve as a vegetable side dish or as a vegetarian entree.

1 large spaghetti squash
1 teaspoon extra-virgin olive oil
1 garlic clove
1 bell pepper, diced (any color)
1 cup sliced mushrooms
1 teaspoon dried leaf oregano
1 teaspoon dried leaf basil
1 teaspoon dried leaf thyme
1 cup water
Dash of salt and black pepper
1 tomato, chopped
1 (4-oz.) can ripe olives, sliced
1 tablespoon chopped fresh parsley

YIELD 4 (1-cup) servings
1 serving = 1 starch, 1 vegetable, and 1 fat

STIR-FRY VEGETABLES

Heat oil, soy sauce, lemon juice, pepper flakes, water, ginger root, and garlic in a large skillet or wok. Add sturdy vegetables first (carrots, green onions, daikon, broccoli stems, bell peppers) and cook 2 minutes. Next add softer vegetables (mushrooms, snow peas, broccoli flowerets, bok choy) and stir-fry another 4 minutes. Vegetables should be crisp-tender.

YIELD 6 (3/4-cup) servings

1 serving = 1 vegetable

2 teaspoons extra-virgin olive oil or sesame oil

1/4 cup reduced-sodium soy sauce

1 tablespoon fresh lemon juice

1/2 teaspoon crushed red pepper flakes

1/2 cup water

2 teaspoons grated ginger root

1 garlic clove, chopped

Assorted chopped vegetables of choice (6 cups): carrots, green onions, daikon, green/red bell pepper, bok choy, water chestnuts, mushrooms, snow peas, or broccoli flowerets

Grains & Starches

BARLEY

Preheat oven to 375°F. Melt margarine in a small skillet. Add onion and cook about 5 minutes or until onion is tender. Place in an ungreased 1-1/2-quart casserole dish. Stir in remaining ingredients, cover, and bake, stirring once, until barley is tender, about 1-1/4 hours.

YIELD 6 (1/2-cup) servings

1/2 cup serving = 1 starch

1 tablespoon margarine

1 medium-size onion, chopped

3-1/4 cups boiling water or vegetable stock

1 cup barley

2 teaspoons vegetable bouillon granules (optional)

1/2 teaspoon salt

BULGUR

Toast cracked wheat in a dry skillet over medium heat 3 to 5 minutes, stirring often. Stir in water or vegetable broth and onion. Cover and simmer 20 to 25 minutes or until liquid is absorbed. Season with salt, if desired.

1 cup cracked wheat

2-1/4 cups water or vegetable broth

1 medium-size onion, chopped

1/2 teaspoon salt (optional)

YIELD 6 (1/2-cup) servings

1 serving = 1 starch

KASHI

Combine all ingredients in medium-size heavy saucepan. Bring to a boil. Reduce heat, cover, and cook 30 minutes or until tender. Kashi can be used as side dish or breakfast cereal.

YIELD 4 (1/2-cup) servings

1 serving = 1 starch

1 cup Kashi®

2 cups water or
vegetable broth

LEMON RICE

Bring broth, salt, and garlic to a boil in a heavy saucepan. Stir in the rice, cover, and simmer until the liquid is absorbed, about 20 minutes. Remove from heat and stir in the lemon peel and let stand, covered, 5 minutes. Remove the garlic. Gently stir in the dill and margarine. Season to taste with pepper. Serve immediately.

YIELD 8 (1/2-cup) servings

1 serving = 1 starch

2 cups chicken broth

1/2 teaspoon salt

1 garlic clove,
slightly crushed

2 cups long-grain
white rice or
Basmati rice

1 tablespoon finely
grated lemon peel

1 tablespoon
chopped fresh dill

1 tablespoon
margarine

Freshly ground
pepper to taste

REEN RICE

Combine chiles, cilantro, and 1 cup of the stock or water in a blender or food processor fitted with the metal blade; process until puréed. Heat oil in a medium-size saucepan over medium heat, add onion and garlic; cook until softened, stirring constantly. Add rice and cook 2 minutes, stirring constantly. Stir in chile purée. Reduce heat to low and cook, stirring, until liquid is almost absorbed by rice. Stir in remaining stock. Cover and cook on low heat 30 minutes or until rice is tender and stock is absorbed. Season with salt and pepper.

4 poblano chiles, roasted and peeled (page 150)

1 cup lightly packed cilantro

4 cups vegetable stock or water

1 tablespoon vegetable oil

1 medium-size onion, chopped

2 garlic cloves, minced

2 cups long-grain white rice

Salt and pepper to taste

YIELD 9 (1/2-cup) servings
1 serving = 1 starch

VARIATION
Use large green chiles instead of poblano chiles.

MULTI-
GRAIN
PILAF

Bring 1 cup chicken broth to a boil and add rice and rye or oats. Reduce heat, cover, and simmer 45 to 60 minutes or until tender. Meanwhile, toast millet lightly in skillet over low heat, stirring constantly. Heat 1/2 cup chicken broth in a small saucepan and add millet. Bring to a boil. Reduce heat, cover, and simmer 25 minutes or until tender. Melt margarine in a medium-size skillet. Add minced onion and cook until softened. Stir in rice mixture, millet, garlic, green onions, tamari, herbs, and Vege-Sal. Keep warm or refrigerate and reheat. Grains may be prepared a day ahead.

YIELD 5 (1/2-cup) servings

1 serving = 1 starch

1-1/2 cups chicken broth

1/4 cup long-grain brown rice

1/4 cup whole oats or rye

1/4 cup millet

1 teaspoon margarine

1/4 cup minced onion

1 garlic clove, minced

1/4 cup chopped green onions

1 tablespoon tamari

1 tablespoon parsley, chopped

1/8 teaspoon rubbed sage

1/8 teaspoon rosemary

1/8 teaspoon Vege-Sal®

ORZO RISOTTO

Melt margarine in a medium-size saucepan with a lid. Add onion and celery and cook until softened. Stir in orzo and toast slightly. Bring water and stock to a boil in a small saucepan and pour over orzo and onion. Stir once and cover. Cook 15 minutes over very low heat. *Do not stir.* Lift lid and check for doneness. It should be tender and slightly moist. As orzo sits, it absorbs water.

YIELD 5 (1/2-cup) servings
1 serving = 1 starch

1/2 tablespoon margarine
1 small onion, diced
1/2 celery stalk, diced
1-1/4 cups orzo pasta
1 cup water
1 cup chicken stock

COUSCOUS

Combine couscous, salt, water, margarine, and curry powder in a large bowl. Let stand 2 to 4 minutes or until water is absorbed. Garnish with parsley.

YIELD 8–10 (1/2-cup) servings

1 serving = 1 starch

2-1/2 cups fast cooking couscous

1 teaspoon salt

2 cups boiling water

1 teaspoon margarine

1 teaspoon curry powder

Fresh parsley, chopped

COUSCOUS WITH MARINADE

Heat olive oil in a medium-size skillet. Add garlic, herbs, onion, lemon peel, and vinegar. Stir in cooked couscous. Heat until hot, stirring.

YIELD 4 (1/2-cup) servings

1 serving = 1 starch

1 teaspoon extra-virgin olive oil

1 garlic clove, minced

1/4 cup fresh mint, minced

2 tablespoons fresh parsley, minced

1 tablespoon chopped green onion

1 teaspoon grated lemon peel

1 teaspoon vinegar

2 cups cooked couscous

1 pound dried black beans

1 tablespoon margarine

1 tablespoon extra-virgin olive oil

1/4 large onion, chopped

2 garlic cloves, minced

1/4 celery stalk, chopped

1 tomato, diced

1 teaspoon cumin powder

1/2 teaspoon red (cayenne) pepper

Black pepper

Salt

Cover beans with water in a large pan and soak overnight. Drain. Put beans back in pan and cover with fresh water. Bring to a boil and boil 10 minutes. Reduce heat, cover, and simmer, stirring occasionally, until beans are very soft and water is mostly gone, about 2 hours. Mash the beans. Heat the margarine and oil in a large skillet. Add onion, garlic, and celery. Cook until tender, stirring occasionally. Stir in mashed beans. Add tomato and seasonings to taste. Cook until mixture is heated through, stirring constantly.

YIELD 6 servings

1 serving = 3 starches and 1 fat

CARIBBEAN BLACK BEANS

2 cups dried black beans

1 medium-size onion, chopped

2 or 3 garlic cloves, minced

2 celery stalks, chopped

2 carrots, diced

2 or 3 tomatoes, chopped

1 cup orange juice

Juice of 1 lime

1/4 cup diced, canned mild green chiles

3 tablespoons chili powder

2 teaspoons ground cumin

1/4 cup minced cilantro

1 teaspoon salt (optional)

Mock Sour Cream (page 37) (to garnish, optional)

Chopped onion (to garnish, optional)

Cover beans with water in a large pan and soak overnight. Drain. Put beans back in pan and cover with fresh water. Bring to a boil and boil 10 minutes. Reduce heat, cover, and simmer, stirring occasionally, until beans are very soft and water is mostly gone, about 2 hours. Add remaining ingredients, except garnish, and cook 30 to 40 minutes, uncovered. If at any time the beans get too dry, add more water or stock to prevent burning. Ladle into a serving bowl and garnish with a dollop of sour cream and sprinkle with chopped onions, if desired.

YIELD 15 (1/3-cup) servings

1 serving = 1 starch

Combine cornmeal, flour, salt, fructose, and pepper in a medium-size bowl. Combine egg yolk, milk, margarine, and corn in a small bowl and add to dry ingredients. Mix until combined. Beat egg white in a small bowl until stiff but not dry. Fold into batter. Heat oil in a medium-size skillet over medium heat. Drop batter by spoonfuls onto hot skillet. Cook until bubbles form on surface. Turn and cook about 2 more minutes or until browned on edges. Can be made in advance and reheated in a moderate oven.

YIELD 4 servings

1 serving = 2 starches and 1 fat

VARIATION

Blueberry Cakes: To serve for breakfast, substitute 1/4 cup fresh blueberries for corn.

2/3 cup blue cornmeal

1/2 cup unbleached all-purpose flour

Pinch of kosher salt

Pinch of granulated fructose

Pinch of white pepper

1 egg, separated

1/2 cup skim milk

1 teaspoon margarine, melted

1/4 cup cooked whole-kernel yellow corn

1 or 2 teaspoons vegetable oil

OVEN-ROASTED NEW RED POTATOES

Preheat oven to 400°F. With a paring knife, remove a 1/2-inch-wide ring of the peel from each potato. Combine remaining ingredients in a medium-size bowl. Add potatoes and toss until well coated. Place potatoes in a baking pan, spray with nonstick cooking spray, and roast 45 to 60 minutes or until tender and browned. Remove from pan, leaving the drippings in the pan.

8 to 12 new red potatoes

1 tablespoon cider vinegar or tarragon vinegar

1/2 teaspoon each of dried leaf basil, thyme, oregano, and tarragon

1/2 teaspoon pepper

YIELD 4–6 (1/2-cup) servings
1 serving = 1 starch

VARIATIONS

Use large russet potatoes, cut into wedges lengthwise, and continue as above. Substitute other vegetables such as carrots, fennel roots, turnips, or parsnips.

Grilled Vegetables: Use seasoning mixture to marinate vegetables. Slice eggplant, zucchini, or yellow squash 1/4 inch thick, dip into the marinade, and grill 2 to 3 minutes on each side.

$\mathscr{P}$OTATO PANCAKES

3 cups finely grated
potatoes

2 eggs, slightly
beaten

1/2 cup unbleached
all-purpose flour

1/4 cup grated onion

1 teaspoon salt

1/4 teaspoon white
pepper

Juice of 1/2 lemon

1 garlic clove,
crushed (optional)

Yogurt and chives
or applesauce
(to serve)

Combine all ingredients, except yogurt and chives or applesauce, in a
medium-size bowl and mix well.
Spray a nonstick skillet lightly with
nonstick cooking spray. Heat skillet
over medium heat. Add 1/2 cup of
the potato mixture to skillet. Brown
well on both sides. Repeat with remaining batter, 1/2 cup at a time,
spraying pan as necessary. Serve immediately. Top with yogurt and
chives or the applesauce.

YIELD 8 pancakes

1 serving (1 pancake) = 1 starch

VARIATION

Sweet Potato Pancakes: Substitute 1
cup grated carrots and 1 cup grated
sweet potato for 2 cups of the grated
potato. Add a dash of nutmeg and
1/4 cup finely chopped parsley. Continue as above.

POTATO-TURNIP SCALLOP

Preheat oven to 300°F. Combine skim milk, sour cream, onion, and parsley in a small bowl; set aside. Scrub potatoes and, if necessary, peel. Slice potatoes and turnips very thin. Parboil or steam them together 4 minutes. Drain well and pat dry with paper towels. Combine flour with seasoning. Spray an 8-inch-square casserole dish (or equivalent) with nonstick cooking spray and dust with flour. Layer half of the potatoes and turnips in prepared dish. Sprinkle with half of the flour mixture. Add another layer of potatoes and turnips. Sprinkle with remaining flour mixture. Pour milk mixture over top. Cover and bake 40 minutes. Remove cover and top with cheese. Bake 20 minutes or until browned and vegetables are tender.

2 cups skim milk

1/2 cup light sour cream

1 green onion, diced

1/4 bunch parsley, chopped

3 medium-size potatoes

3 large to medium-size turnips, peeled

1/4 cup unbleached all-purpose flour

2 tablespoons Mrs. Dash® or Vege-Sal®

1 cup shredded lowfat cheese (your choice)

YIELD 6 servings

1 serving = 1 protein, 1 starch, and 1 vegetable

TWICE-BAKED POTATOES

Wash and scrub the potatoes. Bake in a preheated 350°F oven 60 to 75 minutes or until soft. Remove and let cool. With a serrated knife, cut a 1/2-inch slice off the long side of each potato. With a small spoon, scoop the potatoes out leaving a 1/4-inch-thick wall. If you like a smooth filling, place the potato pulp with the cheeses, sour cream, salt, and pepper in a food processor and process until smooth. Combine with remaining ingredients. Otherwise, place the potatoes in a bowl and mash, then stir in remaining ingredients. Stuff the potato mixture back into the hollow shells, mounding each potato with the stuffing. Place in a baking dish and bake 25 to 35 minutes or until tops are brown.

4 large russet potatoes

1/2 cup lowfat cottage cheese

1/2 cup shredded lowfat Cheddar cheese (2 oz.)

1/2 cup light sour cream

1/2 teaspoon salt or to taste

1/4 teaspoon ground white pepper or to taste

1/2 cup diced onion

2 garlic cloves, crushed

3/4 cup broccoli flowerets

1/2 cup grated carrots

YIELD 4 servings

1 serving = 1 protein and 2 starches

SWEET-POTATO & APPLE SCALLOP

Preheat oven to 350°F. Spray a 1-quart casserole dish with nonstick cooking spray; set aside. Bake sweet potatoes in their skins on a baking sheet 45 minutes or until soft. Cool and peel. Thinly slice apple and potatoes. Place alternate layers of sweet potatoes and apple in prepared casserole dish. Combine honey, salt, ginger, margarine, water, and orange juice in a small saucepan. Boil 3 minutes. Pour over apple and potato mixture. Bake 30 minutes or until apple is tender.

YIELD 6–8 (1/2-cup) servings
1 serving = 1 starch

2 medium-size sweet potatoes
1 apple
1 teaspoon honey
1 teaspoon salt or to taste
1 teaspoon ground ginger
1 teaspoon margarine
1/4 cup water
1 tablespoon orange juice

Heat olive oil in a medium-size skillet. Add onions and livers and cook until livers are cooked through. Add spinach and cook to wilt. Remove from heat. Add dill weed, bread crumbs, salt, and pepper. Allow to cool. Use as stuffing for poultry or seafood (page 45). Omit livers if using with seafood.

1 teaspoon extra-virgin olive oil

4 green onions, diced

4 ounces chicken livers, cleaned and chopped

2 cups packed fresh spinach, chopped

1 teaspoon dill weed

1 cup bread crumbs

Salt and pepper to taste

YIELD 4 servings

1 serving = 1 protein and 1 starch (with livers)

1 serving = 1 starch (without livers)

Breads

ANANA-RAISIN MUFFINS

Preheat oven to 350°F. Spray 8 muffin cups with nonstick cooking spray or line cups with paper cup liners. Combine all ingredients in a medium-size bowl. Stir only until moistened. Pour batter into prepared muffin cups. Bake 20 to 25 minutes, or until a toothpick inserted in muffin centers comes out clean.

YIELD 8 servings
1 muffin = 1 starch and 1 fat

1 cup rolled oats

1 cup whole-wheat flour

1 tablespoon baking powder

1/2 teaspoon ground cinnamon

1 cup mashed bananas (about 2 ripe bananas)

1/4 cup vegetable oil

1 egg, slightly beaten

Preheat oven to 350°F. Spray 12 muffin cups with nonstick cooking spray or line cups with paper cup liners. Beat margarine, eggs, yogurt, and vanilla in a medium-size bowl until combined. Mix dry ingredients in another medium-size bowl. Mash bananas and add to margarine mixture. Add dry ingredients and stir just until combined. Stir in nuts. Do not over mix. Spoon batter into prepared muffin cups, filling almost to the rims. Bake 15 minutes, or until a toothpick inserted in muffin centers comes out clean.

YIELD 12 muffins

1 muffin = 2 starches and 2 fats

3/4 cup margarine, softened

2 eggs, slightly beaten

1/2 cup plain nonfat yogurt

1 teaspoon vanilla extract

3/4 cup granulated fructose

2 teaspoons baking powder

3/4 teaspoon baking soda

3 cups all-purpose flour

Pinch of salt

1/2 teaspoon ground cinnamon

2 medium-size bananas

1/2 cup chopped nuts

BLUEBERRY MUFFINS

Preheat oven to 325°F. Spray 12 muffin cups with nonstick cooking spray. Combine milk, oil, and eggs in a medium-size bowl; add blueberries. Combine flours, fructose, baking powder, lemon peel, and salt in another bowl. Add egg mixture to dry ingredients and stir just to combine. Do not over mix. Spoon or pour batter into prepared muffin cups, filling almost to the rims. Bake 10 to 15 minutes or until a toothpick inserted in muffin centers comes out clean.

YIELD 12 muffins

1 muffin = 2 starches and 1 fat

1 cup skim milk

1/4 cup vegetable oil

3 eggs, slightly beaten

3 cups blueberries, thawed and well drained, if frozen

1-1/2 cups plus 2 tablespoons whole-wheat flour

1-1/2 cups plus 3 tablespoons unbleached all-purpose flour

1/2 cup granulated fructose

1 tablespoon baking powder

1 tablespoon grated lemon peel

1/2 teaspoon salt

ZUCCHINI-
GINGER
MUFFINS

3 eggs, slightly
beaten

1/2 cup margarine,
softened, or
vegetable oil

2-3/4 cups grated
unpeeled zucchini

1 tablespoon grated
orange peel

2-1/4 cups
unbleached
all-purpose flour

1/2 cup granulated
fructose

1 tablespoon baking
powder

1 teaspoon baking
soda

1/2 teaspoon kosher
salt

1-1/4 teaspoons
ground ginger

1/2 cup nuts
(optional),
coarsely chopped

Preheat oven to 350°F. Spray 12 muffin cups with nonstick cooking spray.
Combine eggs, margarine or oil, zucchini, and orange peel in a medium-
size bowl. Combine flour, fructose,
baking powder, soda, salt, and ginger
in another bowl. Add egg mixture to
dry ingredients and stir just to combine. Stir in nuts. Do not over mix.
Spoon or pour batter into prepared
muffin cups, filling almost to the
rims. Bake 15 minutes or until a
toothpick inserted in muffin centers
comes out clean.

YIELD 12 muffins

1 muffin = 2 starches and 2-1/2 fats
(with nuts)

1 muffin = 2 starches and 2 fats (without nuts)

CATHRYN'S COCONUT-CARROT MUFFINS

Preheat oven to 325°F. Spray 12 muffin cups with nonstick cooking spray. Cream fructose and margarine in a medium-size bowl. Stir in eggs, carrots, milk, and vanilla. Combine flours, baking powder, soda, salt, and cinnamon in another bowl. Add egg mixture, raisins, and coconut to dry ingredients and stir just to combine. Do not over mix. Spoon or pour batter into prepared muffin cups, filling almost to the rims. Bake 10 minutes or until a toothpick inserted in muffin centers comes out clean.

YIELD 12 muffins

1 muffin = 1 starch, 1 fruit, and 2 fats

HINT

To toast coconut, spread a thin layer of coconut on a baking sheet. Bake in a 350°F oven 3 to 4 minutes or until lightly browned.

1/3 cup granulated fructose

1/2 cup margarine

3 eggs, slightly beaten

2-1/2 cups grated carrots

1 cup skim milk

1 tablespoon vanilla extract

1 cup unbleached all-purpose flour

1 cup whole-wheat flour

1 tablespoon baking powder

3/4 teaspoon baking soda

3/4 teaspoon salt

1 teaspoon ground cinnamon

1 cup raisins

1/4 cup shredded coconut, toasted

Preheat oven to 400°F. Spray 8 muffin cups with nonstick cooking spray. Melt margarine in a small skillet over medium heat. Add bell pepper and cook until softened. Combine egg, buttermilk and cooked pepper in a small bowl. Combine cornmeal, flour, baking powder, soda, and salt in a medium-size bowl. Add egg mixture to dry ingredients and stir just to combine. Do not over mix. Spoon or pour batter into prepared muffin cups, filling almost to the rims. Bake 10 to 15 minutes or until a toothpick inserted in muffin centers comes out clean.

YIELD 8 muffins

1 muffin = 1 starch and 1 fat

2 tablespoons margarine

1 cup chopped red bell pepper

1 egg, slightly beaten

1 cup buttermilk

1-1/2 cups cornmeal

1 cup whole-wheat flour

1 teaspoon baking powder

1-1/2 teaspoons baking soda

1/8 teaspoon salt

GREEN-CHILE CORN BREAD

Preheat oven to 400°F. Place the 2 tablespoons margarine in a 1-1/2-quart casserole dish or a 9-inch skillet. Place in oven until margarine is melted, but not browned. While margarine is melting, combine corn, eggs, milk, the 1/3 cup melted margarine, chiles, and half of the cheese in a medium-size bowl. Combine cornmeal, soda, and salt in another bowl. Add dry ingredients to corn mixture. Mix until combined but do not over mix. Pour mixture into the warm casserole dish and sprinkle the top with the remaining cheese. Bake 40 minutes or until bread begins to pull away from edges of pan and a toothpick inserted in center comes out clean. Serve hot with a spoon.

YIELD 8 servings

1 serving = 2 starches and 2 fats

2 tablespoons margarine

1 (8-oz.) can cream-style corn

2 eggs, slightly beaten

3/4 cup skim milk

1/3 cup melted margarine

1 (4-oz.) can chopped green chiles

3/4 cup shredded lowfat sharp Cheddar cheese (3 oz.)

1 cup yellow cornmeal

1/2 teaspoon baking soda

1/4 teaspoon salt

1 tablespoon
granulated
fructose

1 envelope active dry
yeast (about
1 tablespoon)

1/2 cup lukewarm
water

1 cup lukewarm skim
milk

1 egg, slightly
beaten

1/4 cup margarine,
softened

About 3-1/2 cups
unbleached
all-purpose flour

1/2 cup whole-
wheat flour

1/4 teaspoon salt

Dissolve fructose and yeast in the water in a large bowl. Let stand 10 minutes or until foamy. Stir in milk, egg, margarine, and about 2 cups of the all-purpose flour and the whole-wheat flour, and salt. Stir in enough of the remaining flour to make a moderately stiff dough. Turn out dough on a floured surface and knead until smooth and satiny. Spray a large bowl with nonstick cooking spray and add dough to bowl. Cover and let rise in a warm place about 1 hour or until doubled in size. Spray a baking sheet with nonstick cooking spray. Punch down dough, divide into 15 equal pieces, and shape into rolls. Arrange rolls on prepared baking sheet, cover, and let rise 10 more minutes or until almost doubled in size. Preheat oven to 375°F and bake the rolls 15 to 20 minutes or until lightly browned.

YIELD 15 medium-size rolls

1 roll = 2 starches

VARIATIONS

If desired, substitute more whole-
wheat flour for some of the all-purpose flour, use honey instead of
fructose or add raisins or cinnamon
for sweeter rolls. The dough can also
be rolled flat and used for pizza crust.
If you have a heavy-duty electric
mixer, the dough can be mixed and
kneaded using the mixer.

Sauces & Marinades

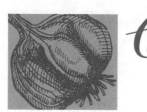

CHIHUAHUA SALSA

Mix all ingredients together in a medium-size bowl. Cover and refrigerate until used.

YIELD 5 cups
1 serving (1 tablespoon) = 1 free exchange
1/2 cup = 1 vegetable and 1 fat

VARIATION
Coarsely chop all vegetables, then process with remaining ingredients in a food processor fitted with the metal blade.

1 cup fresh lemon juice

1/4 teaspoon dry mustard

1/4 cup extra-virgin olive oil

1/2 cup vegetable stock

2 green bell peppers, minced

2 red bell peppers, minced

2 packages radishes, minced

6 green onions, minced

2 tablespoons minced, seeded jalapeño chile pepper

2 tablespoons fresh lime juice

SALSA FRESCA

Peel, seed, and dice tomatoes. Remove seeds and ribs from jalapeño; finely dice. Combine all ingredients. Marinate 1 hour or more. Serve with Quesadillas (page 89), Blue Corn Cakes (page 124), broiled meat, fish, or chicken.

4 Roma (plum) tomatoes

1 medium-size jalapeño chile pepper

1/4 cup cilantro leaves, chopped

2 tablespoons red wine vinegar or apple cider vinegar or 1 tablespoon balsamic vinegar

YIELD 1 cup

1 serving (1 tablespoon) = 1 free exchange

1/2 cup = 1 vegetable

HINT

How to Peel and Seed a Tomato: Remove tomato core and make a small X on the bottom of the tomato with a sharp knife. Bring 1 quart of water to a boil. Prepare a bowl of iced water and keep at the side of the stove. Drop tomatoes into boiling water 1 or 2 minutes or until the skin splits. Immediately transfer tomatoes to the iced water. Allow to cool. Remove from iced water and peel. Cut tomatoes in half crosswise and gently squeeze seeds out of the tomatoes.

WARM DESERT WILLOW SALSA

Combine tomatoes, onion, chiles, and picante sauce in a medium-size saucepan. Season with garlic, cilantro, salt, pepper, and chili powder. Simmer until thickened.

YIELD 6 cups

1 serving (1 tablespoon) = 1 free exchange

1/2 cup = 1 vegetable

1 (15-oz.) can whole tomatoes, blended

1 (15-oz.) can diced tomatoes, drained

1 onion, diced

1 (4-oz.) can green chiles, chopped

1/4 cup bottled picante sauce

1 garlic clove, crushed

1 tablespoon fresh cilantro, chopped

Salt and pepper to taste

1/2 teaspoon chili powder

ENCHILADA
SAUCE

Heat water or broth in a medium-size saucepan over medium heat. Add onion and cook until softened. Stir in remaining ingredients and bring to a boil. Let simmer for 5 minutes. Serve over burritos or cooked chicken.

YIELD 2 cups

1 serving (1 tablespoon) = 1 free exchange

2 tablespoons water or broth

1/4 cup green onion, chopped

1/4 cup green pepper, chopped

2 tablespoons green chiles, chopped

2 teaspoons chili powder

2 (8-oz.) cans tomato sauce

1/8 teaspoon ground cumin

1/2 tablespoon all-purpose flour

PRICKLY-PEAR & ANCHO-CHILE GLAZE

Preheat broiler. Place garlic, onion, and tomatoes, if using, on a broiler pan. Broil until browned. Transfer to a blender or food processor fitted with the metal blade. Add remaining ingredients. Process 30 seconds. Transfer to a medium-size saucepan and heat until warm. Brush on meat before and during grilling.

YIELD 6 cups

1 serving (2 tablespoons) = 1/2 fruit

4 garlic cloves

2 cups finely diced onion

6 tomatoes or 2 cups tomato sauce

1-1/2 cups prickly pear jelly

1 cup apple cider vinegar

3 to 4 tablespoons imitation maple syrup (sugar free)

1/4 cup Worcestershire sauce

1 teaspoon salt

2 teaspoons Dijon-style mustard

1/4 cup puréed ancho chiles

Purée in a blender until smooth. Pour into a saucepan and warm slightly.

YIELD 1-1/2 cups
1 serving (2 tablespoons) = 1 free exchange

HINT

4 red bell peppers, roasted, peeled, and seeded

How to Roast, Peel, and Seed a Pepper: Gas stovetop method: Using long-handled tongs and wearing an oven mitt, grasp a medium-size, smooth as possible, red pepper. Hold pepper over open flame, rotating as needed. Allow pepper skin to blacken. Transfer to a brown paper bag and steam 30 minutes. Remove pepper from bag and rub away the skin under gentle running water. Tear open pepper and pull off stem. Rinse away seeds.

Broiler method: Place peppers on a baking sheet and place under broiler. Remove when pepper skin begins to blacken. Rotate peppers. Continue until peppers are well blackened all around. Continue as above.

RED PEPPER SAUCE

Roast and peel bell peppers according to directions on opposite page. Chop peeled peppers. Mix all ingredients together in a small bowl. Sauce can be used on fish or vegetables.

YIELD 2 cups

1 serving (1 tablespoon) = 1 free exchange

4 red bell peppers

1 medium-size onion, chopped

1 garlic clove, minced

1 jalapeño chile pepper, seeded, and chopped

1 tablespoon extra-virgin olive oil

1 tablespoon fresh lemon juice

1 tablespoon red wine vinegar

Combine basil, garlic, and walnuts in a blender or food processor fitted with the metal blade. Process until chopped. With motor running, slowly add oil. Add cheeses, salt, and pepper. Process to combine. Use on sandwiches. Brush on broiled chicken the last 10 minutes of cooking time. Add 1 tablespoon to 4 eggs as you scramble them.

2 cups packed fresh basil

4 large garlic cloves

1/2 cup walnuts

1/4 cup extra-virgin olive oil

1/2 cup grated Parmesan cheese

1/4 cup grated Romano cheese

Salt and pepper to taste

YIELD 1-1/2 cups or 12 (2-tablespoon) servings

1 serving (2 tablespoons) = 2-1/2 fats

VARIATIONS

Add 1/4 cup evaporated skim milk and use as a pasta sauce. Combine 2 tablespoons pesto, 1/4 cup crème fraîche, and 1 tablespoon Dijon-style mustard to make a sauce for poached fish. Pine nuts can be substituted for walnuts.

SOY-GINGER MARINADE

Whisk together all ingredients in a small bowl. Cover and let stand at room temperature 1 hour to combine flavors before using. Use for grilled chicken and grilled zucchini.

YIELD About 1/2 cup

1 serving (1 tablespoon) = 1 fat (if consuming as a sauce).

1 serving = 1 free exchange (if using as a marinade)

1/4 cup soy sauce

2 tablespoons vegetable oil

1 teaspoon dry mustard

3/4 teaspoon grated ginger root

3 garlic cloves, finely chopped

2 green onions, sliced

1 small jalapeño chile pepper, seeded and chopped

2 tablespoons water

TOMATO VINAIGRETTE

Cook tarragon in vinegar in a small non-aluminum saucepan 1 minute. Combine with remaining ingredients and refrigerate overnight. Serve with grilled chicken, fish, or with buttery cheeses. Use 1 tablespoon vinaigrette as a garnish.

1 tablespoon dried leaf tarragon

1/4 cup tarragon vinegar

1-1/2 cups diced fresh tomatoes or canned tomatoes

2 tablespoons coarsely chopped fresh herbs (basil, marjoram, thyme)

1 large shallot, minced

2 tablespoons extra-virgin olive oil

YIELD 2 cups

1 serving (2 tablespoons) = free exchange

1/4 cup = 1 fat

Desserts

RICOTTA CHEESECAKE

Preheat oven to 350°F. Spread ricotta cheese in a glass pie pan. Cheese will be about 1/2 inch thick. Bake for 35 minutes or until top is golden and firm. Cool to room temperature and spread with blueberry sauce.

YIELD 8 servings

1 serving = 1 protein and 1 fruit

1 pound part-skim ricotta cheese, drained

1 cup Sue's Best Blueberry Sauce (page 158)

SUE'S BEST BLUEBERRY SAUCE

2 cups blueberries

2 cups apple juice

Dash of ground cinnamon, if desired

2 tablespoons cornstarch

2 to 4 tablespoons cold water

Add blueberries to a small saucepan. Bring to a boil and then set aside. Heat apple juice in a medium-size saucepan and reduce to 1 cup. Add cinnamon, if desired. Combine cornstarch and cold water in a small bowl. Add approximately 2 tablespoons of warm apple juice to cornstarch paste and mix. Stir cornstarch/juice mixture into remaining juice, then add berries. Bring to a boil and heat 1 minute. Allow to cool before spreading over the cheesecake.

YIELD 6 (1/2-cup) servings

1 serving = 1 fruit

CARROT CAKE

Preheat oven to 325°F. Spray an 8″x 4″ loaf pan with nonstick cooking spray. Combine flour, soda, and cinnamon in a large bowl. Stir in carrots, pineapple, and walnuts. Mix egg whites, oil, yogurt, honey, and vanilla in another bowl. Pour yogurt mixture into flour mixture and mix well but do not beat. Pour into prepared loaf pan and bake 30 to 35 minutes or until a toothpick inserted in the center comes out clean and dry.

YIELD 6 to 8 servings
1 serving = 2 starches and 1 fat

1-1/2 cups whole-wheat flour

1/2 teaspoon baking soda

1/2 teaspoon ground cinnamon

1/2 cup grated carrots

1/4 cup finely chopped pineapple

2 tablespoons chopped toasted walnuts

3 egg whites

2 tablespoons vegetable oil

3 tablespoons nonfat yogurt

3 tablespoons honey

1/2 teaspoon vanilla extract

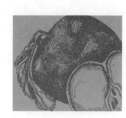

Preheat oven to 350°F. Spray a 12″ x 9″ pan with nonstick cooking spray. Combine the flour, fructose, and cocoa in a medium-size bowl. Stir in margarine and applesauce. Add vanilla and walnuts and stir. Batter will be crumbly. In a separate bowl, beat egg whites until stiff but not dry. Fold whites into batter. Pour into pan and bake 20 to 23 minutes. To test for doneness, insert toothpick into center. Remove brownies from oven if toothpick comes out with small round pieces of brownie on it but not if toothpick is smeared with batter.

2 cups whole-wheat flour

3/4 cup granulated fructose or 1-1/2 cups sugar

6 tablespoons unsweetened cocoa powder

1/4 cup diet margarine, melted

3/4 cup unsweetened applesauce

1 teaspoon vanilla

1/2 cup walnuts, chopped

8 egg whites

YIELD 40 brownies (2-inch squares)
1 serving = 1 starch

VARIATION

To eliminate theobromine (caffeine like substance) in the recipe, 1/4 cup carob may be substituted for the cocoa.

PEAR-CHERRY CRISP

Preheat oven to 400°F. Slice pears. Place in a large bowl with cherries. Add the 1 tablespoon fructose and lemon juice and stir to combine. Using a pastry blender or 2 knives, combine margarine, flour, granola, the 1/4 cup fructose and the cinnamon. Place fruit in the bottom of a 9-inch glass pie plate or an 8-inch-square baking pan. Cover fruit with topping and bake 30 minutes or until top is browned.

YIELD 12 servings

1 serving = 1 starch, 1 fruit, and 1 fat

VARIATION

Apple-Cherry Crisp: Substitute 8 medium-size apples, sliced, for pears.

8 medium-size pears

6 cups whole pitted cherries (thawed frozen, or fresh)

1 tablespoon granulated fructose

1 teaspoon fresh lemon juice

1/4 cup margarine

1/2 cup unbleached all-purpose flour

1 cup granola (your choice of flavor)

1/4 cup granulated fructose

1/2 teaspoon ground cinnamon

BAKED APPLES

Preheat oven to 375°F. Wash and core apples. Set in a nonstick baking pan. Put 1 teaspoon raisins and a cinnamon stick into each apple. Combine the apple juice and water. Pour over apples. Dust the tops of apples with the spices. Cover and bake 30 minutes or until apples are tender.

YIELD 6 servings

1 apple = 1 fruit

6 baking apples
(Granny Smith)

1/3 cup raisins

6 cinnamon sticks

1/2 cup frozen
unsweetened
apple juice
concentrate and
1/2 cup water or
1 cup
unsweetened
apple juice

1/8 teaspoon grated
nutmeg

1/8 teaspoon ground
cinnamon

1/8 teaspoon ground
cloves

1/8 teaspoon ground
cardamom

MOCHA PUDDING CAKE

Preheat oven to 350°F. Spray an 8-inch-square baking pan with non-stick cooking spray. Combine flour, 1/2 cup of the fructose, the 1/4 cup cocoa, the coffee granules, baking powder, and salt in a medium-size bowl. Stir well. Combine milk, oil, and vanilla in another bowl. Add to dry ingredients and stir well. Spoon batter into preprepared pan. Combine remaining 1/4 cup fructose with the 2 tablespoons cocoa and sprinkle over batter. Pour boiling water over batter (do not stir). Bake for 30 minutes or until cake springs back when lightly touched in center. Serve warm topped with yogurt, if desired.

YIELD 9 servings
1 serving = 2 starches and 1 fat

VARIATION

To eliminate theobromine (caffeine like substance) in the recipe, 1/4 cup carob (3 tablespoons in batter and 1 tablespoon in topping) may be substituted for the cocoa.

1 cup unbleached all-purpose flour

3/4 cup granulated fructose, divided

1/4 cup plus 2 tablespoons unsweetened cocoa powder, divided

1-1/2 tablespoons instant decaffeinated coffee granules

2 teaspoons baking powder

1/4 teaspoon salt

1/2 cup skim milk

3 tablespoons vegetable oil

1 teaspoon vanilla extract

1 cup boiling water

1 cup plain nonfat yogurt (optional)

CREAM OF WHEAT PUDDING

2 cups skim milk

1/2 cup Cream of Wheat® cereal, uncooked

2 tablespoons granulated fructose

4 egg yolks, slightly beaten

1/4 cup chopped pistachios or almonds

3 egg whites

Simple Fruit Jam (page 8)

Bring milk to a boil in a medium-size saucepan. Stir in cereal and fructose. Simmer until thickened, stirring frequently. Remove from heat, cool slightly, and stir in egg yolks and nuts. Beat the egg whites in a medium-size bowl until stiff but not dry. Fold one-third of the beaten whites into the cereal mixture, then fold in the remaining egg whites. Transfer to one large or 6 small bowls. Top with fruit jam. Refrigerate until set.

YIELD 6 servings

1 serving = 1 protein, 1 starch, and 1 fat (excluding fruit sauce)

Appendixes

Ingredients 167

Tools for Healthy Living 173

Ingredients

ACHIOTE PASTE A paste made from ground annatto seeds, cumin, oregano, garlic, black pepper, and salt.

Can be purchased in most Mexican food stores or may be special ordered from "La Perla" of Costa Mesa, CA (714) 557-5151.

A substitute for achiote is "adobo" sauce which is most often available in specialty markets in the Mexican food section. Achiote paste is stored at room temperature in an airtight container and keeps several weeks. Adobo sauce comes in a glass jar and, unopened, has a long shelf life.

CAJUN SPICES A mixture of several peppers, cumin, garlic, and oregano. Can be made up from the various spices or purchased in most supermarkets under a name such as "Cajun spice blend" or "Cajun seasonings." Look for blends without salt. Store up to six months at room temperature. Flavor will decrease with longer storage.

CAROB POWDER Made from the ground seeds of the pod of the carob bean tree. Can be found in health foods store, natural foods stores and some supermarkets. Most often used as a substitute for chocolate. Carob is sugar and caffeine-free. Store as you would cocoa powder and when substituting, use 2/3 the amount of carob that you would if using cocoa as the flavor of carob is stronger than cocoa.

CHILES AND PEPPERS At Sierra Tucson we use a lot of canned, roasted Anaheim (green) chiles for our Mexican dishes and some of our salsas. We also use fresh jalapeño chiles for salsa and to flavor guacamole and some other Southwestern dishes that we make here. When using fresh chiles, they should be purchased when they have good color and the skin is tight and without blemishes. Handle fresh and canned chiles carefully and avoid touching your eyes, nose, or mouth while and just after handling them as contact with the fiery juices is most uncomfortable.

For dried chili powders we buy a light chili powder and a dark red chili powder and use the two together to create a mix. Dried chili powders from New Mexico are superior in flavor and freshness but are often hard to find in the stores or through the conventional purveyors. Again, dried chili powders will lose their potency after several months and should be replaced or you may need to use double the amount to reach the level of flavor you'd like for your dish.

ROASTED BELL PEPPERS are available in jars or you can roast them yourself (page 150). The peppers are mild and sweet.

POBLANO CHILES are a moderately spicy pepper. Spicier than canned chiles.

JALAPEÑO CHILES are a spicy chile pepper.

ANCHO CHILES are dried Poblano chiles.

CRÈME FRAÎCHE

CRÈME FRAÎCHE is heavy cream that has been thickened by fermenting with bacteria similar to that in sour cream or buttermilk. Crème fraîche can be boiled without curdling. It is available in specialty markets or can be made at home.

FLOURS

UNBLEACHED WHITE FLOUR is available in all grocery stores, we prefer unbleached flour for the flavor and reduced additives.

WHOLE-WHEAT FLOUR is available in any grocery store; to purchase an organic flour you may need to visit the health foods or natural foods market. Many of our muffin recipes are made with a combination of white and whole-wheat flours for the purpose of lightening up the recipe with the white flour while retaining the bran and germ in the wheat flour. Whole-wheat flour contains more fiber than white flour.

SIFTED WHOLE-WHEAT FLOUR is like using white flour only without all the additives and whitening processes used on the standard white flours. It has little bran or germ remaining which makes it a good natural substitute in dishes like soups and sauces where you want the thickening qualities of the flour without the flecks of bran and germ.

SIFTED WHOLE-WHEAT PASTRY FLOUR is best used in baking cakes and cookies. This flour, like the sifted whole-wheat flour, has little bran or germ visable and also contains less gluten, which is the element in flour that gives it its elasticity. The reduced gluten content makes for a more desirable texture when baking desserts, pie crusts, confections, etc. These last two flours are most likely only found in a natural foods store. All flours should be stored in an airtight container in a cool dry place.

FRUCTOSE A sweetener made from granulated fruit sugars. Fructose is sweeter than processed white sugar (sucrose) and when adapting recipes that call for white sugar, use 1/2 the amount of fructose. Fructose is absorbed into the body a little more slowly than white sugar and does not induce insulin production in the body as does white sugar. Consequently, foods containing fructose are less likely to cause wide swings in blood sugar. Fructose is available in most natural foods stores and may be available in the specialty section of some markets. Fructose is very susceptible to clumping when it comes into contact with moisture and should therefore be stored in an airtight container in a dry place. Fructose will become hard and form a rock if not used in a few weeks time, so buy in small quantities.

GRAINS

COUSCOUS are small pearls of pasta made from finely milled semolina wheat. Whole-wheat couscous is also available. Couscous can be found in the international section of supermarkets or Greek stores.

KASHI® is a mixture of oats, rice, rye, barley, wheat, triticale, buckwheat grains, and sesame seeds. It can be found in the natural foods section of grocery stores. Kashi can be cooked as a side dish or hot cereal.

BARLEY is a sweet grain. Pearled barley has been hulled and the bran has been removed. This lowers the fiber content, but allows it to be cooked more rapidly.

BULGUR (cracked wheat) is a product of wheat berries that have been precooked, dried and cracked. It is available at natural food stores and in international sections of supermarkets.

ORZO is a very small rice-shaped pasta that can be found in most supermarkets.

LONG-GRAIN BROWN RICE has a slightly higher fiber content and more flavor than white rice. Now found in most supermarkets.

MILLET is a yellow, hulled grain that is bland in flavor. Millet can be combined with cheeses, chiles, or other seasonings. It is more perishable than other grains and should be refrigerated in a tightly closed container.

BLUE CORN MEAL is a cornmeal made from blue corn. It can be used in place of yellow corn meal. Blue corn meal can usually be found in natural food stores or in the international sections of supermarkets.

JAPANESE BREAD CRUMBS are a flake-style white bread crumb that is particularly light and adheres well to batter-dipped fish and vegetables. It is available in oriental food sections of some markets or in an oriental specialty foods store.

MOLE PASTE is a blend of ground spices, chiles, and chocolate found in Mexican foods markets or possibly in the specialty foods section of a good supermarket. The brand we prefer is "dona Maria" and comes in an 8-ounce glass jar. Mole, unopened, keeps for several months and after opening will keep in the refrigerator for two or more weeks.

HERBS AND OTHER SEASONINGS We recommend purchasing spices and seasonings in bulk from a natural foods store. By purchasing small amounts, the spices will be fresh and robust with flavor. The natural foods stores also carry a larger selection than supermarkets.

THE FOLLOWING IS A LIST OF UNIQUE HERBS USED IN THIS COOKBOOK.	
CAYENNE PEPPER, GROUND	finely ground dried red pepper made from various dried chiles. Cayenne adds bite to various dishes. Use sparingly.
CORIANDER SEED, GROUND	dried seeds of the coriander plant. It adds a sweet flavor to foods. It is popular in Indian foods. Ground coriander should be used within a couple of months.
CILANTRO (CORIANDER LEAVES/ CHINESE PARSLEY)	imparts a distinct fresh green aromatic flavor for a Mexican touch. Fresh cilantro is far superior to dried cilantro and can be found in the produce section of most supermarkets.
GARLIC	the most pungent member of the onion family. Fresh garlic has a better flavor than granulated. If using granulated garlic, substitute 1/4 teaspoon for 1 garlic clove.
GARAM MASALA	an Indian blend of seasonings. Available in most supermarkets or natural foods stores.
HUNGARIAN PAPRIKA	made from dried, ground, sweet peppers.
KOSHER SALT	coarser in texture and less salty in flavor than "table salt." It is preferable in cooking and has no additives.
SUMMER SAVORY	an herb with a flavor similar to thyme although it is milder.
TURMERIC	a powdered spice used in Indian and Middle Eastern cooking. It imparts a golden color and slightly musty flavor to dishes. It is inexpensive and usually substituted for saffron for coloring dishes, although they have very different flavors.

DRIED HERBS should be added to a recipe early in the cooking process so the herbs will rehydrate and the flavor can develop. Dried herbs are stronger in flavor than fresh herbs and so the quantity of fresh herbs that you may substitute for dried herbs should be about double that of the dried herb. Dried herbs should be purchased in small quantities and used up as soon as possible as they will decrease in potency over time.

FRESH HERBS should be added to a cooked recipe towards the very end of the cooking process as their flavor will cook out if boiled or sautéd too long and more herbs will need to be added to reach the desired flavor. Fresh herbs should be purchased and used the same day and therefore bought in small quantity. If you do find that you have over bought fresh herbs you may tie the remainder with thread and hang the herbs to dry in a warm dry place.

NUTRITIONAL YEAST Contains dried yeast, niacin, Vitamin B1, Vitamin B2, and Vitamin B12. It has a cheesy/nutty flavor. Can be added to beverages, etc. to enhance their nutritional value.

PICANTE SAUCE A blend of tomatoes, peppers, onions, vinegar, salt, and spices. Available in mild, medium, and hot varieties. Used to enhance Mexican dishes.

PROTEIN POWDER A powder usually containing protein from soybeans or milk. Can be mixed with flour for baking or blended in drinks to provide added protein.

SESAME OIL Oil extracted from sesame seeds. Has a nutty flavor and is tasty in salads and for sautéing vegetables. Most often used in oriental dishes and found with oriental foods in the store. Use in small amounts.

TAMARI is a by-product of the miso-making process and is naturally fermented. It is similar to soy sauce, but stronger in taste. Use to add flavor to oriental dishes and salad dressings. Can be found in oriental or natural foods stores. Do not confuse with "tamari soy sauce." Also available in a "light" variety which contains less sodium.

TOFU is fresh soybean curd, very high in protein. Tofu is bland in flavor but absorbs flavors easily. It is often used as an alternative to meat. Tofu can be purchased in differing degrees of firmness, depending on its use. The firmer the "cake" of tofu, the higher the nutrient content. Tofu can be purchased in most supermarkets. After purchasing tofu, it should be refrigerated in water that is frequently changed. It will keep for up to a week.

TEMPEH Contains fermented soybeans which have been formed into a cake. It can also be made of seeds, grains, and other beans. Tempeh

is more flavorful than tofu and can be used as a meat substitute in many dishes as it is a good source of protein. Tempeh is sold, either fresh or frozen, in natural food stores. If purchased frozen, it is best to slice or cube it when it is partially thawed so that it does not crumble.

STOCKS OR BROTHS Are used as bases for many dishes. Chicken, beef, and vegetable stocks are sold canned as broth or as bouillon cubes or granules and can be substituted for homemade stocks, but are usually high in sodium. There are broths available in natural foods stores or some supermarkets that do not have salt added or have less salt than standard products. Bouillon cubes can contain high levels of sodium as well as monosodium glutamate (MSG). Natural foods stores do sell "natural" bouillon cubes without the salt and MSG.

VEGETABLE OILS All vegetable oils are free of cholesterol, but vary in the type and amounts of fatty acids they contain. Two of the vegetable oils are particularly high in monosaturated fats which are believed to lower blood cholesterol levels. These are olive oil and canola (rapeseed) oil. Other vegetable oils that are high in polyunsaturated fats, but not as high in monosaturated fats as these two, are safflower, sunflower, corn, soybean, and sesame oils.

Tools for Healthy Eating

COMPONENTS OF EATING IN RECOVERY

Healthy eating is an important part of recovery. Listed below are some suggestions to remember as you progress on your journey.

SUGAR It is best to keep the simple sugar content of the diet low. High-sugar foods containing honey and table sugar (sucrose) are usually empty-calorie foods, meaning that they supply little nutritional value other than calories. High-sugar foods are commonly binge foods for people with eating disorders and other addictions.

When blood sugar drops, it has to be replaced by a meal or snack. A poor choice is a food high in simple sugar, such as a candy bar or soda. A better choice is to eat a complex carbohydrate, such as crackers, with some protein and fat, such as cheese or peanut butter. This helps the body balance the blood sugar levels and prevents a rapid rise in blood sugar followed by a sharp decrease.

CAFFEINE Caffeine is an addictive substance that can cause rapid heart rate and abnormal heart rhythms. It is also a mild diuretic, which may cause water loss from an already depleted system, causing dehydration. Caffeine stimulates acid production in the stomach, which adversely affects gastric problems such as ulcers, gastritis, and heartburn. Caffeine also causes blood sugar to drop leading to feelings of hunger. Finally, too much caffeine can cause headaches, nervousness, and difficulty sleeping.

BALANCED MEALS Eating three balanced meals a day is important for several reasons. Consuming adequate amounts of food at mealtime may prevent some people from overeating between meals, especially in the afternoon and evening. Skipping meals earlier in the day often leads to overeating later on. The result of overeating at dinner or later in the evening often is skipping breakfast the following morning, and the pattern continues.

Eating three balanced meals a day is also important for weight management. Skipping meals can lower the metabolic rate so the body does not burn as many calories. Additionally, three balanced meals are important for maintaining sustained energy levels. Skipping breakfast and lunch and eating a large meal later in the day is comparable to putting gas in a car at the end of the trip. Finally, people usually make healthier food choices for meals than for snacks. Filling up at meals on healthier foods is preferable to snacking on foods such as chips and candy that contain a lot of calories, fat, and sodium, but minimal nutrients.

Meals need to be balanced with respect to carbohydrates, proteins, and fat. A good rule of thumb is to have a protein food, a starch food, and a fruit and/or vegetable at each meal. The protein food will provide protein and some fat in addition to vitamins and minerals. The starch food will provide mostly complex carbohydrates, perhaps a small amount of fat, vitamins, and minerals. Fruits and vegetables are good sources of vitamins, minerals, and carbohydrates, including fiber.

CARBOHYDRATES It is recommended that most dietary calories come from carbohydrates. Complex carbohydrates should comprise 50 to 60 percent of one's total calories. Examples of complex carbohydrate foods include: legumes (beans, peas, and lentils) whole grains (rice, millet, bulgur, oats, and barley), pasta, potatoes, whole-grain foods (cereals and bread), fruits, and vegetables.

Complex carbohydrates offer many healthful benefits. It is a myth that carbohydrates are "fattening." Carbohydrates have the same calories per gram as proteins, but less than half the calories of one gram of fat. Complex carbohydrates are rich sources of vitamins and minerals, including thiamin (B1), folate, iron, and niacin. Complex carbohydrates are an important source of fiber. Fiber helps to satisfy the appetite, keeps the digestive tract running smoothly, helps prevent constipation and helps maintain normal levels of blood sugar and cholesterol. Carbohydrates are the body's main energy source. Carbohydrates break down to glucose, which is the main fuel for the brain and muscles. Without adequate carbohydrates, the body will use its own protein for energy.

Simple carbohydrates such as the sugars found in candy, sodas, and

174

cookies are less nutritious than complex carbohydrates. These foods are high not only in sugar but many are also high in fat.

PROTEIN Most Americans eat at least twice as much protein as they need. Excess protein is stored in the body as fat. Eating excess protein can put a strain on the kidneys, because they have to filter out the waste products from protein breakdown. Ideally, 20 percent of total calories should come from lean protein sources (low in fat).

Protein foods include fish; poultry; meat; eggs; dairy products such as cheese, yogurt, and milk; dried beans and peas; peanut butter and tofu. Animal proteins such as fish, poultry, meat, eggs, and dairy products are complete proteins (These contain all the essential amino acids.) They provide balanced protein which the body can use to meet its needs. Proteins from non-animal sources, such as dried beans and peas, nuts and vegetables, are by themselves incomplete protein. Incomplete proteins need to be combined daily with other complementary proteins to form complete proteins. The following is a chart on how to combine complementary proteins:

When eating legumes, including any of the items in section B of this chart will complement the protein in legumes in section A.

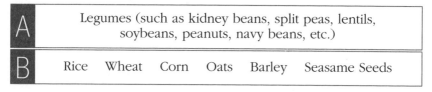

A	Legumes (such as kidney beans, split peas, lentils, soybeans, peanuts, navy beans, etc.)
B	Rice Wheat Corn Oats Barley Seasame Seeds

A moderate protein intake (20 percent of calories) is important because every cell in the body contains some protein. Protein is part of muscle, bone, skin, blood, and antibodies that fight illness, among other things. The body's cells are constantly dying and being replaced, and good-quality proteins are essential for this turnover. Choose lowfat sources of protein because many protein sources are high in saturated fat.

FAT Most Americans consume an excess amount of fat. A high-fat diet can contribute to obesity, heart disease, and certain types of cancer. Fat contains over twice as many calories per gram as proteins and carbohydrates. Calories from fat are also converted to body fat more readily than calories from proteins or carbohydrates. Excluding all fat from your food is also not healthy, however, since some fat is important for vital organs, cell membranes, vitamin absorption and energy. Having some fat as part of a meal helps with satiety. The key is moderation.

In order to reduce fat intake, the following changes are suggested:

◆ Eat leaner protein sources such as fish, skinless chicken, or turkey breast, and very lean, trimmed cuts of beef (round, sirloin, or loin), or pork loin. Broil, grill, or bake instead of frying in fat.

- ◆ Choose lowfat dairy products such as skim or lowfat milk, part-skim cheeses, nonfat, or lowfat yogurt, and lowfat cottage cheese.
- ◆ Add less fats to food. Cut down on the use of margarine, oils, and salad dressings. Limit or avoid foods with cream sauces.
- ◆ Don't overdo nuts, seeds, and avocados.
- ◆ Limit chips and desserts. Most ice cream, chocolate, candy, pies, cakes, cookies, doughnuts, and pastries are high in fat.
- ◆ Avoid foods that have been fried.

FLUIDS Water is an important nutrient. The body is actually composed of about two-thirds water. Every cell in the body depends on water to function properly. Water helps eliminate waste products, helps in food digestion and lubricates the joints. An adequate water intake, along with high-fiber foods, helps to eliminate constipation.

Thirst is an indication of fluid needs, but the body is actually somewhat dehydrated by the time thirst is experienced. To keep up with fluid needs, particularly in warm weather, it is recommended that eight to ten 8-ounce glasses of water be consumed daily. Other beverages such as herb teas, juices, and milk can count as fluids, but try to make water the primary fluid.

Soft drinks should be limited as a fluid source. Regular soft drinks are just empty calories. They contain water, artificial colorings and flavorings and sugar. A 12-ounce can of soda contains 9 teaspoons of sugar. All this sugar actually increases the body's need for water. Diet soft drinks, although sugar free, are not a healthy alternative. Scientists do not fully understand the effects of aspartame (Nutrasweet™) on the human body.

EATING ON THE RUN
Healthy Fast Food

It is sometimes difficult to eat healthy as part of a busy schedule. Nutrition still needs to be included, especially during busy times. The following section provides some ideas to make it easier to eat healthy as part of a busy life style.

MEAL PLANNING TIPS

- Refer to "Shopping List Staples" (page 181) for basic food items to keep on hand.

- Brainstorm for ideas for meals you would like to have in the next week. Include others in your household for their ideas. Write down meal ideas and post the list on the refrigerator or bulletin board.

- Consult newspaper for sale items that you wish to include in your meal planning (optional).

- Narrow list down to five to seven entrees that you will prepare for the next week.

- Consider which entrees can be prepared in bulk and frozen for future use. This saves preparation time.

- Consult recipes to determine which ingredients you will need; inventory to see which ingredients you have on hand and then write your shopping list for the ingredients you need to purchase.

- If applicable, consult your meal plan to determine which other foods you will need to purchase for the week (fruits, dairy, vegetables, grains).

SHORT CUTS FOR PREPARATION OF QUICK AND EASY MEALS

- Make extra and freeze some. This works great with soups, pasta sauce, broth, casseroles, lasagna, etc. Just make a large quantity, divide what you don't need into small containers and freeze.

- A slow cooker can save valuable time. Put soup ingredients into the cooker before you leave for work. When you get home, supper is ready. For beans, soak overnight and in the morning pour off the soaking water. Cover with fresh water and turn on the slow cooker.

- Make extra of basic foods you use often and keep them in the refrigerator. Extra cooked rice or grains, partially cooked pasta, pasta sauce, baked potatoes, etc., can usually be microwaved for a spur-of-the-moment quick meal. Soak and cook a large pot of beans (2 to 4 cups at a time) and freeze in quart-size containers for future use. Thaw in the refrigerator or microwave.

◆ Use very fresh ingredients so leftovers will last. Dishes like stuffed potatoes, dairy-based dressings, etc. can be refrigerated and used for later if all ingredients, especially dated ones, are fresh to begin with.

◆ Plan ahead. Be sure you have all the ingredients on hand and know what you're going to do. It's less stressful than coming home from work at 6 o'clock and having given no thought to dinner.

◆ Incorporate leftovers. They're already cooked. Add a few new ingredients, seasonings, or condiments, and you have a new dish.

◆ Keep some healthy "convenience" foods on hand for emergencies. These could include some of the frozen or packaged entrees that are low in fat, sodium, and calories.

◆ Keep a variety of frozen vegetables on hand. These save time in numerous recipes, from soups to stews to stir-fry.

QUICK BREAKFAST IDEAS

FRUITS

◆ Add variety by serving different combinations of fruit juices such as:

Cranberry juice cocktail with pineapple, grapefruit, apricot, or orange juice

Orange juice with grapefruit juice, prune, grape, pineapple, or loganberry juice

Pineapple juice with apricot or pear nectar

Apple juice with grape or cranberry juice

◆ Serve pieces of fruit in a fruit juice such as:

Orange juice with grapes, grapefruit sections, or sliced bananas

Pineapple juice with orange cubes or sections, sliced bananas or grapefruit sections

◆ Combine two kinds of fruit such as:

Sliced peaches with raspberries

Sliced bananas with strawberries or blackberries

Applesauce with diced pears

Dried prunes cooked together with dried apricots

Squeeze lime wedges over chunks of fresh papaya.

Sprinkle chopped nuts over grated raw apple.

- Serve a mixed fruit cup with cottage cheese or yogurt topping.
- Serve a chilled grapefruit half with only a sprinkle of salt.
- Top fresh apple slices with peanut butter.
- Serve combination milk and fruit drinks.

CEREALS

Cook cereals in nonfat (skim) milk instead of water.

Add a bit of toasted wheat germ to cooked cereal.

Add a cup of fruit to hot cereal a few minutes before serving. Unsweetened canned fruits such as peaches are just as tasty as the more commonly used dates and raisins.

Serve hot cereal around a steaming baked apple.

Add chopped nuts to either cooked or dry cereal.

Top hot cereal with orange or apple juice instead of sugar and milk.

Stir peanut butter into hot cereal and top with chilled applesauce.

Cook whole grains overnight in an electric slow cooker for a hot, tasty ready-to-serve dish.

Serve leftover rice heated with a dash of cinnamon, raisins, or chopped apple and skim milk.

BREADS

Make toast in different shapes from bread baked in large juice cans, pie plates, large and small loaf pans, square, or round cake pans.

Serve waffles with fruit or unsweetened fruit toppings.

Try a sandwich for breakfast instead of lunch with whole-grain bread or whole-grain pita with lowfat meats or lowfat cheese.

Serve toast or bagel with part-skim ricotta cheese.

PROTEIN FOODS

Serve an egg omelet using eggs or egg substitute with tomato, lowfat cheese, mushrooms, and fresh vegetables.

Top waffles with chili beans.

Serve cottage cheese or part-skim ricotta cheese topped with berries or other fruits.

Serve peanut butter on toast, waffles, or bagels, and top with strawberries, raspberries, applesauce, or sliced bananas.

Serve a high-protein soup of lentils, split peas, or garbanzo beans.

Serve a scrambled egg with fresh vegetables in a whole-grain pita.

QUICK LUNCHES

Portioned leftovers in microwavable-containers and fresh fruit, bread/lowfat crackers, beverage (water, iced tea, milk).

Sandwich—choose any combination below, put in separate plastic bags or containers the night before, and it's ready to go.

◆ Sliced lean meat, lowfat tuna salad, lowfat cheese

◆ Tomato slices, lettuce, sprouts, sliced zucchini

◆ Bagel, bread, pita bread

Yogurt (with fresh fruit or sweetened with fruit juice), bagel, fruit, and raw vegetables (this is really quick).

Leftovers that are ideally suited for lunch: spaghetti, stew, soup, chili, stir-fry vegetables with rice, casserole, pasta salad.

QUICK SUPPERS

Prepare as much as possible the evening before or in the morning. Prepare sauces, chop vegetables, etc. in advance.

Prepare foods in quantity that freeze well (soups, spaghetti sauce, meat loaf, cooked beans, etc.).

Make a pizza with bagels, English muffins, pita bread, or Boboli™ bread. Use lowfat vegetable toppings such as green bell pepper, mushrooms, sliced tomatoes.

Stir-fry vegetables (if vegetables are chopped in advance, or use frozen vegetables) and serve with quick-cooking brown rice (or cook rice in advance). If desired, strips of chicken or lean beef add flavor and protein.

Tostadas: Toast corn tortillas and top with canned vegetarian refried beans, shredded lowfat cheese, chopped tomato, shredded lettuce, and salsa. Serve with rice, fresh fruit, and beverage.

Burritos: Whole-wheat flour tortillas rolled around a mixture of refried beans and salsa. Serve with chopped tomato and shredded lettuce. Use plain yogurt in place of the usual sour cream.

SNACK SUGGESTIONS

Popcorn—air popped (avoid high-fat microwave popcorn)

Lowfat crackers with lowfat cheese or old-fashioned peanut butter

Raw vegetables with lowfat dip

Fresh fruit

Fruit juice sweetened lowfat yogurt or plain lowfat yogurt mixed with chopped fresh fruit (see recipe on page 5).

Whole-grain bagel

Pretzels or "corn chips" (corn tortillas toasted and broken)

Unflavored gelatin sweetened with fruit and fruit juice

Lowfat cottage cheese and fruit

Half a sandwich

SHOPPING LIST STAPLES

FRUITS: fresh, frozen, unsweetened, canned juices

VEGETABLES: fresh, frozen vegetables, and vegetable juices

STARCHES: grains, whole-grain bread, cereal (hot/cold), whole-grain crackers, beans, whole-grain pasta

DAIRY: lowfat or skim milk, nonfat yogurt

PROTEINS: lean meats, cottage cheese, poultry, eggs/egg substitutes, fish, tofu, beans

FATS: margarine, oil, salad dressing

SEASONINGS: garlic, basil, onion, oregano, parsley, bay leaves, lemon/lime, chile peppers, soy sauce, hot pepper sauce

BLENDS: Lawry's Salt-Free 17, Mrs. Dash®, Parsley Patch®, Veg-It®, Vege-Sal®

ADDITIONAL HANDY ITEMS for one-pot meals in a hurry:

canned tomatoes	carrots	frozen chicken breast (skinned)
onions	spaghetti sauce	
tomato sauce	celery	frozen ground turkey
russet potatoes	green bell pepper	frozen ground beef
tomato paste	red bell pepper	frozen fish fillets

LABEL READING

SUGAR First, read the list of ingredients. It is surprising how many forms of sugar are in some foods (fat-free salad dressing, baked beans, canned soup, cereal). Just because there is sugar in a food does not make the food unhealthy; however, if sugar (or a sweetener) is listed as the first, second, or third ingredient, the food may be high in sugar. Some common "sugars" in foods are:

Sucrose

Brown sugar

Raw sugar

Honey

Corn syrup

Dextrose

Fructose

High fructose corn syrup

Concentrated fruit juices/
  natural sweeteners

Maple syrup

Molasses

Mannitol

Sorbitol

Xylitol

Dextrins and maltodextrins

Malt

Some labels give additional "carbohydrate information" that can be helpful in determining the amount of sugar in food. This is common on breakfast cereals, but not many other foods. A general guideline is that if the cereal has more than five grams (about 1 teaspoon) of simple sugar (sucrose) per serving, it is high in sugar.

FAT Many food labels list cholesterol content in addition to amount of total fat, saturated fat, and unsaturated fat content. When watching fat intake due to high cholesterol levels, pay more attention to total fat and saturated fat content than to "no-cholesterol" labelling.

The recommended daily intake of calories from fat is less than 30 percent of daily calories. Not all foods eaten need to be lowfat. Some foods are almost 100 percent fat and are okay in small portions (margarine, salad dressings, avocado, nuts and seeds). The key is balancing portions to eat less than 30 percent of the calories from fat.

A general guideline to evaluate frozen dinners and entrees is to compare total grams of fat to total calories in one serving. For example, if an entree contains 350 calories, then cross off the last number, 35∅, and divide by 3 (35/3 = 11.8). In order to be less than 30 percent fat, this food would need to have less than 12 grams of fat per serving.

When looking at saturated fat, a food is healthier if the majority of the fat comes from unsaturated fat. For example:

- ◆ Total fat grams: 10
- ◆ Saturated fat grams: 3
- ◆ Polyunsaturated and monounsaturated fat grams: 7

RECIPE MODIFICATION

Our favorite recipes are sometimes too high in fat or sugar. Use this list of sug-gestions to help adjust those recipes so that they contain less fat, sugar, and calories.

FAT

◆ When sautéing, leave out the oil or butter and use broth, water, and seasonings or vegetable juice instead.

◆ Use nonstick pans and nonstick cooking spray when browning or sauteing.

◆ Decrease the added fat in most recipes by 1/4 without affecting flavor or quality. If the food is too dry, compen-sate by increasing another liquid ingredient. A pureed fruit such as applesauce or mashed bananas can be added to baked goods to add moisture.

◆ Use leaner cuts of meat and poultry. Trim fat and skin before cooking. Decrease amount of meat in the recipe. Leaner cuts of meat include the tenderloin, loin, and top round. Leaner cuts of poultry include the skinned breast (white meat).

◆ Substitute ground turkey or chicken (no skin added) for ground beef.

◆ Chill soups and stews before serving, skim fat from the top, reheat and serve.

◆ Use milk in place of nondairy creamer or half and half. Even whole milk has less fat than nondairy creamers. Skim milk or skim milk powder is best.

◆ Substitute evaporated skim milk for evaporated whole milk or half and half.

◆ Use plain nonfat yogurt in place of part of the mayonnaise in a tuna or chicken salad.

◆ Use plain nonfat yogurt and/or cottage cheese in place of sour cream and mayonnaise.

◆ Substitute lowfat cottage cheese, part-skim ricotta cheese or tofu in place of mayonnaise or cream cheese.

◆ Add lowfat cheese in place of regular cheese.

◆ Season pasta, rice, potatoes, and vegetables with herbs or flavored vinegars instead of butter and salt.

◆ Substitute two egg whites for one whole egg.

SUGAR

◆ Substitute concentrated fruit juice, fruit, or applesauce for all or part of the sugar in a recipe. Other liquids in the recipe may need to be decreased.

◆ Add cooked fruits to hot cereals to provide sweetness.

◆ Decrease the sugar in most recipes by 1/4 without affecting the flavor.

◆ Substitute granulated fructose or honey for sugar. Use about 1/2 the amount listed in the recipe as fructose and honey are much sweeter than sugar. If using honey, other liquids may need to be reduced.

BASIC MEASUREMENTS

VOLUME

Dash = 6 drops = 1/8 teaspoon

3 teaspoons = 1 tablespoon
= 1/2 fluid ounce

4 tablespoons = 1/4 cup
= 2 fluid ounces

5-1/3 tablespoons = 1/3 cup
= 2-2/3 fluid ounces

8 tablespoons = 1/2 cup
= 4 fluid ounces

16 tablespoons = 1 cup
= 1/2 pint = 8 fluid ounces

1 pint = 2 cups

1 quart = 2 pints

1 gallon = 4 quarts = 16 cups

WEIGHTS

2 ounces = 1/8 pound

4 ounces = 1/4 pound

8 ounces = 1/2 pound

16 ounces = 1 pound

MENU PLANNER

	Monday	Tuesday	Wednesday	Thursday
B R E A K F A S T				
L U N C H				
D I N N E R				
S N A C K				

Friday	Saturday	Sunday	Food Group
			Protein
			Starch
			Fruit
			Vegetable
			Milk
			Fat
			Protein
			Starch
			Fruit
			Vegetable
			Milk
			Fat
			Protein
			Starch
			Fruit
			Vegetable
			Milk
			Fat
			Protein
			Starch
			Fruit
			Milk

Index